Alliance
Academic Review
1998

Alliance Academic Review

1998

Elio Cuccaro, Ph.D.
Editor

Christian Publications, Inc.
Camp Hill, Pennsylvania

Christian Publications, Inc.
3825 Hartzdale Drive, Camp Hill, PA 17011
www.cpi-horizon.com

Faithful, biblical publishing since 1883

ISBN: 0-87509-812-6
©1998 by Christian Publications
All rights reserved
Printed in the United States of America

98 99 00 01 02   5 4 3 2 1

To Alliance academics everywhere
for their contribution
to the advancement
of Christ's kingdom

Contents

Editorial: An Explicit Profession ix

Preface.. xiii

The Journey to an Indigenous Church: The History
    of The Christian and Missionary Alliance Work
    with Native Americans
    Doug Haskins 1

Training Missionaries to Reach Resistant Peoples
    Timothy C. Tennent..31

Premillennialism and the Alliance Distinctives
    Joel Van Hoogen..41

Approximating the Millennium: Premillennial
    Evangelicalism and Racial Reconciliation
    Douglas Matthews 71

Holy Laughter and Other Phenomena in
    Evangelical and Holiness Revival Movements
    Paul L. King 107

Implicit Christians: An Evangelical Appraisal
    K. Neill Foster 123

About the Authors..147

An Explicit Profession

Are all people who do not make an explicit profession of the Christian faith eternally lost? This is arguably the most crucial soteriological question currently debated in books and articles. Dismissing the pluralist option (namely, all religions are a saving way to the one God) as outside the camp, two vying evangelical paradigms have emerged that seem to cross theological traditions, exclusivism and inclusivism. Both agree that Christ is the only salvific way to God, but they disagree as to the specific applicability of the normative standards of salvation. Exclusivism maintains the historical claim of Cyprian and Augustine that outside the Church there is no salvation. The few that are saved out of a condemned world are saved by the one and only method of accepting, by biblical faith, Christ's redemptive work. The hard form of this position would exclude all others from the kingdom of God—pagans, unconverted Jews, children shy of the age of accountability, infants, the mentally challenged, abortions, stillbirths, etc., are all condemned.

A soft form of exclusivism is willing to contend for an exception or exceptions to this normative, one-and-only method. The exception most defended by far is the salvation of the infants of believers. The Roman Catholic Church did it by the sacramental effectiveness of infant baptism. Luther did it by positing a "baby faith" that God received but that men could not outwardly detect. The Reformed tradition has done it by binding the covenantal blessing of salvation to infants through the faith and sacrament of the community of faith, the Church. So while retaining the position of faith in Christ as the only salvific way for adults, the application of this standard to the infants of believers was adapted to their unique circumstances.

Further adaptation to the circumstances of all those who have not or could not hear the gospel of faith in Christ leads some to the position of inclusivism. At the outer end of its argumentation, this position allows that a sincere "implicit faith" on the part of pagans (who have never heard the gospel through no fault of their own) is accepted by God as embracive of Christ. (For a detailed critique of implicit faith, see the last article in this issue.) Thus a few pagans who clung by faith—however minimal by the normative standards—to such a sliver of the true knowledge of God as they had from general revelation are also included in, it is suggested, Christ's salvation.

Inclusivism takes the historical avenue of soft exclusivism to its logical extreme with alarming results. If all the exceptions from the history of mankind are numbered, they would easily make up more than the number of adults that have ever been saved. Now the normative has become the exceptional and the exceptional the normative! This I cannot and will not believe. If the exceptional is more important than the normative, then God's trust to preach the gospel has only vouchsafed to us a minor route to God's heaven. I cannot construe the tenor of Scripture allowing for this.

Clearly the mainline position of the Church has been a conservative soft exclusivism. But given the continuity between this paradigm and inclusivism, how can it persuasively argue against inclusivism's greater willingness to adapt the one-and-only means of salvation to the varied conditions of all humanity? The best it can hope for is a negotiated settlement that somehow would allow the normative way of salvation to retain its ascendancy. To my conscience, this is not good enough.

Perhaps we need to revisit the salvation of the infants of believers. Notice that there are as many explanations for the way of infant salvation as there are theological traditions. For all the extrapolations for the inclusion of our infants (not children) to whom we are emotionally bound, the Scripture teaches that "flesh and blood cannot inherit the kingdom of God" (1 Corinthians 15:50). Certain relevant affirmations have helped me to sift the truth here. God is under no obligation to save anyone or else the fallen angels would also have a chance for salvation (2 Peter 2:4). The unfortunate condition in which mankind finds itself is also a part of the judgement of God against fallen humanity. The gospel is not a panacea for all of mankind; it is "the power of God for the salvation of everyone who believes" (Romans 1:16).

The more that I read about this issue, the more conclusively I am driven to the position of hard exclusivism. This position alone stands only on what can be clearly affirmed by Scripture about God's way of salvation. To answer the question posed at the beginning: as far as the way of God's salvation is committed unto men, we affirm that only those who explicitly believe in the gospel of Christ are saved.

Perhaps, given the current climate of religious pluralism and the uncritical acceptance of every kind of claim regarding religious truth, this paradigm risks making the gospel unduly scandalous to our generation. Inclusivism is so much more in keeping with the spirit of our age, it may be argued. The lesson of history is that the potential for over-accommodation to the cultural expectations of society is a constant threat to the purity of the faith once for all delivered to the saints. Because the application of the very gospel of Jesus Christ is at stake, I want to remain on the safe side of this debate.

God has committed to us the words of life. We can only speak what we know. May God give us the courage not to add or subtract from the one-and-only way of life that He has provided for us in Christ Jesus, our Lord.

Preface

The *Alliance Academic Review*, first issued at Council '95, is an anthology dedicated to and composed mostly by Alliance academics around the world. Comparable writing by other Alliance members is welcomed. The common virtue of all writing shall be that it is consistent with and promotive of the biblical message, the ministry and the mission of The Christian and Missionary Alliance. The *Review* intends to publish, disseminate and keep in print the best work of our academic research.

To be inclusive of all theologically related disciplines, a sincere effort has been made to accept an equal number of papers from the following five academic divisions:

1. Alliance Heritage/Church History
2. Biblical/Theological Studies
3. Church Ministries
4. Missions
5. Religion and Society/Integration of Faith and Learning

Articles submitted may have been recently published elsewhere, recently delivered orally or specifically written for the *Review*. Each is expected to be well-researched, presented and documented. The esoteric and technical should be avoided or, at least, relegated to the endnotes. *The Chicago Manual of Style*, Fourteenth Edition, is the writing style standard. It shall be the responsibility of the writer to secure copyright permission for prepublished material submitted.

Articles and correspondence should be directed to the editor:

Dr. Elio Cuccaro, Senior Editor, CPI
c/o Nyack College, Nyack, NY 10960
Fax: (914) 268-5499
E-mail: Cuccaroe@nyack.edu

The authors of accepted articles will be rewarded with a modest stipend. Articles not chosen will be retained on file for possible future use, unless their return is requested.

As long as the *Review* elicits a favorable response, it will be continued as an annual series.

In This Issue

We lead off with two missions articles. The first by Doug Haskins reviews the history of The Christian and Missionary Alliance work with Native Americans in the United States. He suggests that our meager results are attributable to the failure to establish a truly indigenous Church. The second article by Tim Tennent is concerned with the education of would-be missionaries. He shares the approach of the Toccoa Falls missions program in preparing future missionaries to minister to resistant peoples around the world.

The next two articles draw attention to one of the distinctives of our Statement of Faith: premillennialism. First, Joel Van Hoogen justifies the premillennial stance as the best millennial option. He shows, moreover, that premillennialism is intricately bound to the development and success of our society as well as to our other distinctives and emphases. Second, Doug Matthews makes the case that "commitment to a properly conceptualized earthly utopia negates otherworldliness and . . . affirms that racial reconciliation is the future now."

The penultimate paper by Paul King reprises the authenticity of holiness revival phenomena, such as holy laughter. Renewed interest in this subject has been spurred by the recent manifestations characteristically observed in the "Toronto Blessing." He concludes that the middle ground Alliance position should still be our guide: these phenomena include elements of the genuine and the counterfeit mingled together;

therefore, we should steer clear of condemning them altogether or considering them essential to revival.

Lastly, CPI Publisher K. Neill Foster engages a watershed issue that I also comment on in my editorial: whether salvation is limited to those who place an explicit faith in the preached Christ. An implicit faith in an unpreached, therefore not salvifically known Christ, is found to be "another gospel" that is making serious inroads into Christ's Church.

A final note observes that half of the authors of this issue are pastors, not academicians. May their tribe multiply.

The Journey to an
Indigenous Church: the History of
The Christian and Missionary Alliance
Work with Native Americans

Doug Haskins

In this article I want to review the seventy years of The Christian and Missionary Alliance work with Native Americans, specifically as it relates to the development of a true, indigenous Native Church. I will start with the historical beginnings of this ministry of the Alliance and point out along the way what I believe are some key incidents in the development of the Native Church. This article is being written based on the belief that the best way to reach the Native American today and tomorrow is through a true, indigenous Native Church, functioning within the framework of The Christian and Missionary Alliance.

After I have looked at the history of the work, I will offer some observations I have made or learned from doing the research for this article and from ten years of ministry with Native Americans. It is my hope and prayer that this article can and will be used to strengthen the Alliance work with Native Americans, specifically in the area of moving towards a true, indigenous Native Church.

1

The First Quarter-Century, 1924-1948: The Years of Sacrifice

The mission with Native Americans started from the burden of two single ladies, Miss Belle Thompson and Miss Dorothy Hanley, who were students at St. Paul Bible College in the early 1920s. They went to the northern part of the state of Minnesota and started an outreach among the Chippewa/Ojibwe people on the Leech Lake Reservation at Onigum around 1925.[1] In a few years the work had expanded to include a site on the White Earth Reservation at Naytahwaush started by Floyd Pollock, along with a station at Perch Lake on the Fond Du Lac Reservation in Minnesota by Mr. and Mrs. Puckett. These works were under the leadership of the Northwestern District.

These people were responding to a burden they had from God for the Native American people. They went out as home missionaries with the prayer and moral support from the Northwestern District. The financial support they received was around $20 a month, when the funds were available.

The Lord was moving on the White Earth Reservation. By 1931, the station at Naytahwaush was organized and a new work was opened on the White Earth Reservation with Mr. Swante Lindquist and Mr. Herbert Rupp. The Pollocks moved from the White Earth reservation to the Leech Lake Reservation to the town of Cass Lake to start another site amongst the Chippewa. By 1936, this new mission in Cass Lake was also organized. The ministry had grown in these ten years—there were seventeen workers among the Native Americans at this time, with the majority of them being in Northern Minnesota and a couple in North Dakota.

Growth continued at a fast pace. In 1937, a Chippewa convert from the White Earth Reservation, Mr. Selam Ross and his wife Adeline, began a ministry of evangelism at Squaw Point on the Leech Lake Reservation and in the Vineland area on the Mille Lacs Lake reservation as well as at White Earth. In 1938, a work was started in Fort Totten, North Dakota with the Sioux by Miss Belle Thompson. An additional site on the Leech Lake Reservation was started at Inger by Miss Elsie Rupp.

It was about this time of 1937-38 that another ministry among Native Americans was started in a different area of the country. "Miss Janny Carlyle Hardgraves had a burden for the Lumbee Indians in the Southwest part of the state of North Carolina. E.H. Clemmer picked up this burden and began working with the Lumbees around Lumberton, NC at this time."[2] This effort was under the direction of the South Atlantic District.

The decade of the '40s saw continued growth. It was during these years that many significant happenings took place. In 1943, the building at White Earth burned to the ground, temporarily shutting down the site. In 1944, the Northwestern District saw a need to establish some bylaws specifically for the mission. By 1945, the work had increased to the point that the district realized there was a need for an Indian camp and Bible school. They saw the need to train Native Americans to reach their own people. Forty acres five miles north of Cass Lake had been donated by a Christian Chippewa man, Laverne Bunker, for this purpose. Coupled with this was the recognition of the need for "a man to be appointed by the District Executive Committee to head the Indian work, under the direction of the District Superintendent."[3]

Part of the reason for growth during this decade was the sacrifice and dedication of the workers. The budgeted monthly allowance each worker received during this time from the district was $25. Some months no allowance came and often only a partial allowance was paid out. "In Arlee, Montana, Miss Anna Sontra and Miss Belle Thompson took what they were getting for allowance and used it to purchase 3 lots for $50.00 per lot."[4] It was this willingness to sacrifice and the determination to see the work grow, regardless of the cost, that helped the growth during this time period.

The Golden Years, 1948-1954: The Years of Progress

By 1948 in the Northwestern District, there were fourteen Indian stations with thirty-four workers.[5] The "First Native

American pastor, Selam Ross, was ordained this year."[6] Mokahum Bible School also was started this year along with adult and youth camps for Native Americans on the forty acres of land which had been donated.

The mission was growing, but not without cost.

> Satanic forces oppose advance on every field. Early in the year we found it necessary to remove two of our workers from one of the fields. Drunken children, eight and ten years of age, ripped the screens from their windows because the girls would not let them come into the house. Young men, while under the influence of liquor, broke out six of their window panes, blackened one of the girl's eyes, and upon more than one occasion became so violent that their lives were in danger. . . . The same type of persecution broke out in another field. On the other hand, the blessings of God have rested upon some of the fields in a special manner. Souls have been saved on some, while on others God has given our workers the favor and confidence of the people.[7]

With the "starting of the school the Northwestern District had established a standing committee, made up of people from the Northwestern District, to oversee the Native American work in their district."[8] In "1949 Rev. George French, the dean of men at St. Paul Bible College, was appointed Director of the Indian Work."[9] He served for a year and then "Rev. Keith Bailey in 1950 became the Director of the Indian work and the principal of Mokahum school."[10] The school was seen as the pivotal point for the ministry to continue and to grow. The potential of Native people reaching out to their own people with the gospel message was the driving force behind Mokahum school.

> We are fully persuaded that the Mo-Kah-Um Indian Bible School is in the order of God. When Selam Ross, our faithful Indian brother, visits any of our fields, the

Indians come out to hear him. This proves that genuinely converted, thoroughly consecrated, trained Indians can reach their own people. We would request much prayer, therefore, for faculty and students.[11]

The mission was growing to the point that the Northwestern District was hard pressed to finance it. The main method used for raising support in the district was through offerings taken at youth rallies throughout the district. So "deputational trips outside of the district began about this time to other Alliance works to help in the support of the ministry to the Native Americans."[12]

The years of 1948 through 1954 are seen as the golden years of the mission by many people. "The district was working with people from four different tribes—Chippewa-Oneida-Cree-Sioux—in 11 different reservations. In 1950, seven new workers were added which brought the total up to 40."[13]

The first workers conference was held at Mokahum Bible School in 1950 with representatives from all sixteen stations attending.

The purpose of the conference was threefold. First, to provide a time of spiritual refreshing and fellowship for the missionaries. Secondly, to give the missionaries a better understanding of the needs and problems of other fields. Third, to study proper missionary methods to employ in building a native church among the Indians.[14]

"The predominate [sic] note of the conference was a unified organized effort to evangelize the Indians of the Northwest."[15]

An emphasis was placed upon working in the language of the target people group: "ten missionaries were studying the Chippewa language. In December of 1950, a radio ministry in the Chippewa language was started over the radio station in Bemidji, Minnesota. . . . This ministry was supported by the young peoples group of the Havelock Church in Lincoln, Nebraska."[16]

Also in 1950, "a representative of the American Bible Society spent six weeks with the personnel at Mokahum studying the Chippewa language to arrive at a phonemic alphabet."[17] This led to the beginning of the translation of the book of Mark into the Chippewa language. Coupled with this was "the preparation of a Chippewa primer and the inauguration of a reading campaign."[18] In 1951, a quarterly newspaper was started to give the news, needs and challenges of the American Indian Mission.

This was a time of rapid implementation of new tools and ideas. Some statistical information concerning the work will help in understanding how strong it then stood. At the Northwestern District Conference in 1950, the Director of the Indian mission reported that the total number of established Christians among the Indians was 128. With established Christians being defined as those who had "proven themselves by a consistent Christian walk over a period of months or years."[19] That same year they reported "171 Indians have prayed for the first time."[20]

The goal and dream of the missionaries at this time was that "the Indian Christians would give and serve and propagate the Gospel among their own people."[21] Movement toward this dream becoming a reality was shown statistically: "giving $2,004.20 towards the local expenses of their missions. . . . The total missionary pledge for the Indian fields is $1,215.80."[22]

Two important developments occurred in 1953. One was the establishing of a six-month training program for new missionaries coming into the field held at Mokahum. The missionary candidates would "study the language, get acquainted with the methods and policies of the mission as well as learn to live and work in close contact with the Indian people."[23] The other highlight was "the appointing of one of the graduates of Mokahum Bible School, Mr. John Bobolink, Jr., as a full time missionary. This appointment brought the number of Native Men working full time as Official Workers to three."[24]

The Alliance work with Native Americans was at its high point in 1954, based on number of workers and number of fields: "There were 42 missionaries on 19 mission stations in the Northwestern District."[25] Another radio station was added, carrying the Chippewa broadcast. By this time it had grown to be "the largest Home Mission Development of The Christian and Missionary Alliance."[26] The work was continuing around Lumberton with the Lumbee Indians in North Carolina. It was about this time that "Rev. Eugene Hall started working with E.H. Clemmer in Lumberton. Within a few years the work had moved from an addition on a house to building its own meeting place."[27] In 1955, Mr. and Mrs. Hurd left a mission in Hard Rock on the Navaho reservation in Arizona. They came to Navaho Mountain area in the northwest corner of the Navaho reservation, on the Utah border. "They pitched a tent and started an outreach which would later grow into a church for The Christian and Missionary Alliance with the Navahos."[28]

During this time period of 1948 through 1954, the strategy behind the ministry was becoming more and more indigenous based.

> A very vital part of our Indian Mission is the Bible training school. The future of the Indian church rests upon the success of this venture of faith. Only a well-trained, Spirit filled Indian Ministry can maintain the work already accomplished and continue to propagate the Gospel among their people.[29]

The Loss of Momentum, 1954-1974: The Years of Destabilization

The gap between the strategy and reality of indigenization was already substantial and headed for worse. In 1954 the work closed in North Dakota on the Turtle Mountain Reservation at St. Johns. Rev. Keith Bailey, who appears to be the motivator behind the push for an indigenous church, resigned from his position as Principal of Mokahum and Director of the District's work with Native Americans. During this year there was also a major change in the structure of leadership over the work in the Northwestern District. The "title of Director of the American Indian Work was changed to Secretary, and the District Super-

7

intendent was placed in charge of the Indian Committee instead of the former director."[30]

The ministry had expanded past the limits of its financial resources. In 1954, "there was a severe testing when for a period no allowances were paid."[31] "By 1956, the work had dropped from 19 stations to 13 and from 42 workers to 33."[32] A couple of the workers needed to take leaves of absence for sickness, one for a nervous breakdown. The daughter of the principal of the school was sick and in need of hospitalization which pulled the principal away from his duties at the school. In 1957, she passed away, leaving her parents so distraught that they resigned from the school and moved away. On a more positive note, the District Superintendent of the Northwestern District called for renewed prayer and intercession on behalf of the work. "We must not allow the enemy to destroy this phase (*Native American*) of our work. Problems should be solved, differences put under the blood and together we should expect our best year to produce a strong, vigorous Indian Church!"[33] (italics mine).

It was during this difficult time that "three of the works amongst the Native Americans changed their emphasis of ministry from being 'Indian stations' to 'Anglo churches' at Cass Lake, Minnesota; Bena, Minnesota and Arlee, Montana. At Cass Lake, some of the Chippewa believers stayed with the Cass Lake church. Others moved down to Squaw Point to meet with Chippewa believers there."[34] In Bena, some of the Native believers left the church, holding meetings at Sugar Point. "In Arlee the two single lady missionaries, Miss Belle Thompson and Miss Anna Sontra, moved from Arlee to Ronan, Montana to continue working among the Flathead people."[35]

By the end of the 1950s and the beginning of the 1960s major social changes were taking place that greatly affected the ministry. The termination program of the federal government was being hotly contested because of what it was doing to the Native American people. The state of Wisconsin was hit especially hard by this program because the federal government had picked the reservations in this state to be the first ones to be terminated. During this time, the Northwestern District noticed three trends which were bringing about rapid change in the Native American populations.

1. A steady migration of the Indian population from the reservations to the cities and towns. One-third of all the Indians have left the reservations.
2. Some measure of education is now about universal: 130,000 Indian children and youth attended school last year.
3. The rate of population increase among Indians is more rapid than among white people. The number of Indians in the United States and Canada has doubled in the last sixty years.[36]

In 1961, another call came from the Northwestern District Committee overseeing the Native work to move towards an indigenous church.

> We recommend that a study committee of five, three of which to be Indian workers, be appointed by the District Executive Committee to study methods and policy necessary for the establishing of the indigenous church in Indian work and report back to the 1962 District conference.[37]

It is interesting to note the definition of indigenous church used by the District committee in making this recommendation: "A self-supporting church." This partial definition shows that there were good intentions, but its omission of self-governing and self-propagating suggests some deficiency on the part of the District Indian Committee on what a true indigenous church should be.

This well-intentioned recommendation was voted down by the conference representatives. There was a growing split between District Conference and its right of authority and the people involved in the outreach to Native Americans over the direction the mission should take. This is what the Assistant Director to the District, who was by virtue of his office the Director of the Indian Work, had to say in the conclusion of his report to District Conference the same year it rejected this study commission.

> Each year our Indian Bible School becomes more important to our Indian work. As a trained Indian ministry begins to take responsibility, the results are most encouraging. Our goals for the future should include a steady increase of the percentage of trained Indian pastors and workers. Year after year, our budget for Indian work increases. We must aim for the day of the indigenous church which will increasingly shoulder its own responsibility, support its own trained Indian ministry and govern its own program.[38]

Tension was mounting in the mission during the '60s, mainly over the issue of finances. The district was finding it increasingly difficult to find the funds for the growing budget of the Native American work within its boundaries. In 1962, the Northwestern District Conference passed a recommendation to "appeal to the Home Department for an annual grant of $10,000 from the established Home Mission Fund for the support of our Indian Mission."[39] No funds were sent from the Home Department.

The Northwestern District did see a need for the workers among the Native Americans to have a stronger voice in the decision-making process. So in 1962, they "changed their district constitution governing the ministry amongst American Indians to allow the workers to elect a Field Secretary who would be a member Ex-officio on the District Indian Committee."[40] They also saw the importance of developing and using literature that was specifically geared toward the Native American as a means of outreach. "A budget line item was added by the district in 1963 for this purpose."[41]

However, at the same time as these hopeful steps above, other decisions were being made that were counterproductive to achieving an indigenous church. One was "closing down the six months training program for new missionaries coming into the work in 1964."[42] Another decision involved the reworking of the District Committee overseeing the Indian work. The representation on the committee was not balanced: there were more people on the committee not directly involved in ministry to the Native Americans than there were who were directly involved, and the committee was too large.

> The Committee on Indian Work shall have authoritative control and direction of the work along administrative lines and shall consist of the Director (*Assistant District Director*), the Field Secretary and the Principal of Mokahum Bible School, who shall be members ex-officio. Six additional members shall be elected by the District Prayer Conference for a term of three years; one missionary to the American Indians and one district worker to be elected each year. (italics mine)

was changed to

> ... shall consist of the Director (Assistant District Director), the Field Secretary and the Principal of Mokahum Bible School, who shall be members ex-officio. Four additional members who shall be elected by District Conference for a term of two years; one pastor and one layman to be elected each year.[43]

This helped in cutting the number of people on the committee from nine to seven. But it only made the balance on the committee worse by eliminating the requirement of a missionary working with the Native Americans. This reduced the representation on the committee of people actively involved in the work, while keeping others who were not involved. When the District Committee was reduced in this manner, the District was undermining the need for Native people to be a part of the decision-making process, contrary to the indigenous principles of self-governance.

Another important event which occurred in 1964 was a re-

11

quest from the Indian Workers' Conference in the Northwestern District:

> That the Indian Workers' Conference go on record as favoring nationalization of Alliance Home Missions and that we request the 1964 District Conference of the Northwestern District of The Christian and Missionary Alliance to send a letter to the Home Department of The Christian and Missionary Alliance, expressing this request and calling for positive steps to be taken to effect this at the earliest possible date.[44]

The hope was, that by being nationalized, the ministry would have a larger base of support.

In 1965, the Northwestern District of The Christian and Missionary Alliance was divided up into four different districts. One effect this had on the work with Native Americans was to take four of the existing areas of ministry and move them from the Northwestern District to the control of the Rocky Mountain District (Fort Yates, North Dakota; McLaughlin, South Dakota; Hays, Montana; and Ronan, Montana). Because of this breakup into four different districts, there was further concern over how this might erode the support base for the mission among the Native Americans, unless it was nationalized.

The Home Department of The Christian and Missionary Alliance had sent out a proposed outline of the nationalization of Home Missions. After studying it, the Northwestern District agreed with the reasons for the nationalization of Home Missions:

> 1. WHEREAS the desire to include our Indian Work in a national Home Missions program is based on the very reasons stated in the Home Department paper as the need for nationalization, which are as follows:
>
> 1. Lack of administration
> 2. Failure to employ proper missionary methods

3. Failure to have an indigenous church as a goal
4. Inadequate and inequitable financing
5. Limited promotion[45]

It is the opinion of a number of people involved in this ministry today that these issues remain some of the main problems. The District Executive Committee of the Northwestern District listed three additional reasons for the need to nationalize the outreach among the Native Americans at this time:

WHEREAS other Home Missions have been nationalized by our society, and

WHEREAS the Northwestern District is finding it financially impossible to carry the whole burden of this ministry, and

WHEREAS it seems apparent that the Rocky Mountain District is not able to finance the Indian Work in that area; it is hereby RESOLVED, that the district superintendent inform the Home Secretary of The C&MA that due to these financial problems, we again urge the nationalization of the Indian Work.... [46]

Even during this time of financial stress, a new initiative began which was a step towards developing an indigenous church. In 1965, Rev. Charles Fiero was approached about returning to Minnesota from Canada to head up a literature program to include:

1. Completion of translation of the New Testament and certain portions of the Old Testament (*into Chippewa*)
2. Development of the monthly publication *Truth*
3. Preparation of a hymnbook in the Chippewa language
4. Provide tracts in "Indian English"
5. General translation work
6. Taking charge of Bible correspondence courses

7. Teaching students with an aptitude for literary work (italics mine).[47]

By 1969, out of this literature program had grown a newspaper/magazine for Christian Native Americans called *The Indian Christian*.

By the end of the 1960s, involved people were starting to be discouraged. Forty years of work were completed and there were really no strong churches to point to. The works at Naytahwaush, White Earth and Cass Lake, promising in the late '40s and '50s, now were either shut down or struggling to exist. In 1953, the "largest work amongst the Native Americans was in Oneida, Wisconsin among the Oneida people."[48] By 1970, the station no longer existed.

A number of questions were being asked about the causes of the decline. Three main reasons were given.

1. *Lack of proper methods*, i.e., failing to work towards an indigenous church. "Students from Mokahum Bible School would come back to school saying their home churches would not allow them to be involved in the ministry when they were home."[49]

2. *For almost all of the first forty years, the majority of the workers in the field were single ladies.* These ladies were able to minister to the women and children, teaching Sunday schools and Bible studies with the ladies. They were very active in doing home visitation. "Miss Helen Johnson and Miss Elsie Rupp visited 450 homes their first year in McLaughlin, SD."[50] This isn't speaking against single women missionaries. Without them the Alliance would possibly not have any viable mission with the Native Americans. They responded to the call of God with their lives. Many of the single women were the most dedicated, sacrificing, loving workers on the field. But if you are to build a church, at some point you need to be reaching men. If anything, this speaks against the vision of the organization, not the single women who gave their lives to the work.

3. *The lack of available workers, especially Native American Christian men.* If you are not reaching men, you have a very small pool from which to pull pastors. Many of the stations

died off slowly because no worker could be found to stay and work with the people. Part of this problem of lacking leadership may derive from using the traditional Western approach to training leaders, a Bible school where the students would leave home to be trained. When they came back, many people in the area thought the students no longer fit into the community, thus limiting their ministry.

The Promise of Nationalization, 1975-1997: The Native American District

The '70s was a decade of major change. Responses to the call to nationalize and the three factors above, brought major change in 1975. The work was nationalized as an ethnic district under what was called Specialized Ministries (today it is called Intercultural Ministries), under the supervision of what used to be called the Home Department, now called the Division of Church Ministries.

The strategy of the outreach was to develop an indigenous work. This meant a fresh look at how to develop leaders. Mokahum Bible School had produced some graduates. However, by the '70s only two pastors working in the field had graduated from Mokahum: Rev. Herman Williams and Leonard Fineday. There were other men who were graduates of Mokahum who were pastors, but they were not pastors with the Alliance. In 1975, the "expected enrollment at Mokahum was one student."[51] Whereas in 1970, "there was an enrollment of fifteen students."[52] The "highest number of students to attend Mokahum in a year had been 20, in 1953."[53]

Specialized Ministries decided to use a Theological Education by Extension (TEE) program instead of the Bible school. Mokahum was closed. The hope was that it would be easier to find men willing to be pastors and to be trained if they did not have to leave their home. The training would be more relevant to the specific areas the people were living in. TEE has seen good success with many different ethnic groups, but it has never caught on with Native Americans. From 1975 until 1997, four men have been trained for the pastorate in the Native

American District through the TEE program. Of these four, only one is actively serving in the district in 1997.

From the mid-'70s up through the early '80s, the churches in the newly formed Native American District were learning how to come together and function as a district. By 1978, they had drawn up a set of bylaws for the District to follow.

1. The following committees are set up as standing committees of the Alliance Indian Church Conference: The Budget Committee, Tellers, Evangelism and Church Planting Committee, Conference Committee, Program Committee (Sisseton 1978).
2. Each member congregation in the Alliance Indian Church Conference will be required to support the operation of the field offices and the field executive committee by sending 5% of its total monthly income to the field treasurer.
3. The term of office for members of the field executive committee shall be for two years.[54]

The structural format of the new Native American District was a carbon copy of the structure of a regional district. On the surface the work became indigenized in 1975 by the forming of a Native American District. But structurally nothing had changed. It was still required to function along a Western structure instead of being allowed to develop a structure based on the cultures of the different Indian tribal groups.

These early years gave hope of being indigenous, of being self-governing, for the new district. In 1971, Rev. Herman Williams resigned from his position as principal of Mokahum Bible School and moved back to Arizona to work with his people, the Navaho. He moved to Navaho Mountain where Mr. and Mrs. Hurd had been faithfully carrying on a small ministry with the people.

When Herman arrived, he "stressed indigenous principles from the beginning." [55] "When he was doing home visitation, he would take leaders from the church with him, teaching them how to do visitation." [56] He taught and encouraged the people to be involved in their church, to be active in the church instead of allowing the white people and a few others to do everything. At first it was a struggle, but the Holy Spirit began to move. By 1978, the church had tripled in size, mainly through the application of indigenous principles in the church.

In 1977, another mission group based in Flagstaff, Arizona was struggling with a ministry they had in Shonto, Arizona, which is about fifty miles from Navaho Mountain. "Because of the growth in the work at Navaho Mountain, they offered to turn the Shonto work over to the Alliance. So a Navaho man who was being trained at Navaho Mountain Church, Amos Grass, went to the Shonto church as a pastor." [57]

When the Native American District was formed in 1975, a field executive committee was formed which consisted mainly of Native American men from different churches in the new District. For the first time, the "committee over the work" was Native American instead of Anglo. In 1977, the Field Executive Committee had set a goal "that decisions will be made for the Indian Church by the Indian Committee." In 1979, they learned, "The Field Executive Committee does not have the authority to re-assign personnel when necessary. This responsibility lies with Specialized Ministries Director . . ." [58] In order for the Field Executive Committee to have the final authority in making decisions, the district needed to become a fully organized district. The 1989 edition of the Manual for The Christian and Missionary Alliance set the number of organized churches needed to become an organized district under Specialized Ministries at ten. In the 1995 edition of the Manual, the number of organized churches needed to become an organized district under Intercultural Ministries is forty. Until an ethnic district becomes fully organized, all decisions in the district have to be ratified by the Division of Church Ministries through Intercultural Ministries.

The newly formed District was focusing on growing as fast as it could. The Christian and Missionary Alliance Church as a whole had a campaign going during this time period to double in size by 1987. Likewise, the "Native American District at their District Conference in Aberdeen, SD in 1979 voted to double their constituency and double their number of churches giving them 22 churches."[59]

In 1982, the Native American District set a goal of being fully organized by 1987. This meant going from one organized church at Navaho Mountain to ten organized churches in five years. The District had eleven places where work was going on, but only one was organized as a church at the time. The "qualification to organize as a church was and is to have 20 adult members." [60] By 1985, four other churches had become organized: in 1983, Sisseton, South Dakota; in 1985, Dunsieth, North Dakota, Twin Cities, Minnesota and Mokahum Chapel at Cass Lake, Minnesota. The District has not organized another church since the three were organized in 1985.

One of the hopes for nationalizing the mission was that it would make available more finances to help the work grow. At first this was true, but by the early '80s through General Council action, the process of funding cross-cultural work in the USA was changed, thus limiting available resources. By 1979, the Chippewa Bible broadcast was dropped to one station. By 1982, this ministry was stopped because there was no funding for it. "In 1978, Specialized Ministries decided to reprioritise funding to church planting over auxiliary ministries. Thus funding for the Alliance Indian Publications, the literature work of the District, was stopped by the fall of 1979."[61] This meant stopping the production of the Christian Magazine, the *Indian Christian*. When this decision came down from Specialized Ministries, the publication part of the ministry went independent, relocated to Winnipeg, Manitoba and joined with another magazine called *Indian Life*. Today this ministry is growing as an independent organization called Indian Life. They produce a newspaper called *Indian Life* with an "estimated readership of over 250,000."[62]

The early and mid-'80s were a positive, promising time for the newly formed District. There was progress in becoming indigenous. New works were being started. In 1983, a chart was drawn up which showed the growth of the district towards becoming fully indigenous.

1975	1983
1. Field Committee made up of all but one or two Anglo pastors.	Field Committee made up of all Indians except for one Anglo.
2. The field was dependent totally on outside finances to operate.	Conference churches partially support the conference with ten percent of their total offerings and are working toward full support. The total is $2,448 for the last year.
3. One organized Indian church.	Three organized churches with several more soon to organize.
4. One Indian pastor.	Seven Indian pastors.
5. Missionaries manning all but one mission station or church.	Only two churches led by missionaries.
6. No church building constructed and paid for by Indian people.	Two church buildings constructed and paid for by the people.
7. No new works started by Indian people.	Four works started by Indian people: Tuba City, Paiute Mesa, Bena, Phoenix.
8. Few aggressive plans and goals for church growth.	Preliminary work has been done to begin a number of churches in eastern North Carolina. Goals have been written up to establish works in Denver and Los Angeles. Plans are to have regional divisions in AICC with each region having its own "Regional Director."
9. No ongoing program to train and sharpen the skills of existing pastors.	Quarterly Leadership Training Seminars.
10. Mokahum Indian Bible School.	Field-wide TEE with a full time Field Coordinator.
11. No missionary receiving even partial support from the local congregation. One pastor supported by the congregation.	Ten pastors receiving at least partial support, with all churches working towards full financial independence.[63]

In an effort to see the District grow, to see more churches organized and to finally become self-governing, the Field Executive Committee studied the Native American populations in this country. They recognized the trend of more and more Native Americans moving into urban settings. Demographic study by the Field Executive Committee in 1985 "showed that 53% of the Indian population was under the age of 16." [64] During the 1980s, an emphasis was put on reaching metropolitan areas, with a strong emphasis on young adults. The hope was that the Native American people would be more responsive to the gospel when they had moved into an urban setting.

In 1983, Craig Smith moved to Phoenix, Arizona to start an outreach; in 1988, one was started in Seattle, Washington; in 1989, another was started in Colorado Springs; in 1992, another was started in Portland, Oregon; and also in 1992, an attempt was made to start a work in Albuquerque, New Mexico. Out of these five starts, two are still going today. Phoenix closed in 1994 when the people grew tired of not being able to find a pastor. In 1994, the ministry in Colorado Springs transferred from the Native American District to the Mid-American District, and in 1996 it was decided to move the couple working in Albuquerque to Flagstaff, Arizona.

By 1984, the Field Executive Committee realized that changes were needed in the structure of the District. The geographical distances between churches were too great, and the cost of getting to all the churches was too high to allow for visitation from the leadership in the District. Most of the works were struggling and in need of some guidance and support from the District leadership. In an attempt to help in this area, "the district added an assistant director to be the main person to travel and help the churches in the northern part of the country while the director would travel among the churches in the southern part of the country." [65]

By 1988, they realized this structure wasn't working well either. So they "proposed an Assistant Director in the north and one in the south with a Director overseeing the whole work."[66] The idea was that these three positions would be salaried positions supported by Intercultural Ministries. This plan was not ratified by Intercultural Ministries; thus it was not put into practice.

In 1989, at District Conference, a bold step was taken by the District to "establish a goal of having 70 churches by 1996. The hope was that the Native American District would start about four churches during this time. The other churches, around 40, would come from a joint effort of local Alliance churches in areas with a Native American population working with the District to establish these churches."[67] This goal saw the responsibility of reaching Native Americans resting with both the Native American churches within the Alliance, and the denomination itself. From this goal, three churches were started by the District—Colorado Springs, Colorado; St. Paul, Minnesota and Portland, Oregon. By 1996, only one of these—Portland, Oregon—was still in existence.

By the end of the '80s and the early '90s, frustration was settling in on the leadership in the Native American District: frustration with not being able to come up with finances to support the plans for growth the District had envisioned and frustration from having to have all decisions ratified. In 1991 a study commission formed to look at the way the District was structured and come up with some suggestions. This study committee recommended changing the leadership structure from a western model to a model more like the traditional Native American structure. It was felt by Intercultural Ministries that the structure of the District was too top-heavy, meaning the majority of the funds going into the district were supporting the structure instead of going toward new initiatives. What developed is the Council system the District is functioning under today. The Native churches in different regions of the country gather together forming a regional Council. Each regional Council functions as the Field Executive Committee for that region, with only one Director over the District.

In 1991, when the Council system was introduced, the morale and hope of the District was at an all time low. Discouragement was strong throughout the District. The District Director had just resigned his position. There wasn't a Native American man to take his place, so the District elected a man who had been a missionary for over twenty years. To some this was seen as going backwards, losing what ground had been gained toward being indigenous.

Discouragement was so high during this time that for four

years, no District Conference was held because the churches in the different areas could not agree on a time or a place to meet. God used this time to strengthen the regional Councils by building working relationships between the churches in each regional Council. Each Council decided how often they were going to meet. One chose every other month and another one chose four times a year.

The churches contribute ten percent of what comes into the church to the local Council. This is similar to the ten percent the churches gave to the District under the old system, the difference being that each Council decides how the money collected from the churches will be used in their own area or region. In a few years, the churches saw the money in the Council grow to the point where the Councils were helping churches in need. This has led to a growth in hope for the churches. They are beginning to grasp that God can and will build His Church through them. Yet in going to the regional Council system, a native voice on the national level has been weakened. Some major decisions such as closing a work and how to dispose of items such as chairs, tables and musical instruments, were made by Intercultural ministries without consulting the regional Council.

Some Observations

1. The Native American District in The Christian and Missionary Alliance is quite a way from being truly indigenous. Having their own District, with a Director and a District Conference, does not suffice to make it indigenous. As long as decisions have to be ratified by the Division of Church Ministries, it is not fully an indigenous work. The difficulty does not lie in the desire of the Division of Church Ministries. It is their goal and desire to see indigenization achieved.

The problem is the process to follow in becoming indigenous. Here is where the cultures clash. Western culture says the first step to becoming indigenous is becoming self-supporting. In other words, he who has the money makes the decisions. For the majority of Native American cultures, the right to self-governance is not based on money but on experience and wisdom. In the Western culture, the value of experience and wisdom is based upon the amount of money produced. In Native American cultures, the value of experience and wisdom is based on what has been secured for the community, not the individual.

From the perspective of the Native American District, self-governance needs to be the starting point of the process of developing indigenous churches. This was the first goal set by the newly formed District in 1977. It has yet to happen. To have decisions ratified by outsiders is demeaning, patronizing and similar to treating people like they are children or captives/slaves of war. (In Jesus' day, for example, the Jewish people had to have their major decisions ratified by the Romans.) The time has come to stop relating to the Native Americans as a conquered people.

We need to ask ourselves if we would continue to give money to something over which we did not have the final say. Asking the Native Churches to become self-supporting before they are self-governing is doing just that. Asking them to fund and support methods and structures which they do not relate to is telling them, "This is the direction you will go, and you will pay for it yourselves." Again this is treating them like a conquered people instead of brothers and sisters, equals in Christ. If the Native American work is going to become indigenous, the lesson from history is that it must first become self-governing before it will become self-supporting.

2. Finances have continually been a handicap in the development of the District. Again, this is the area which has been placed first in the process of becoming indigenous. There is some irony here. In establishing a new geographical district in The Christian and Missionary Alliance it is recommended that there be forty churches before a District is formed. This is generally the size needed to support a District. Yet for ethnic districts, they are being told to support financially a district geographically as big as the whole US with as few churches as they have. But they cannot be self-governing until they reach the magical number of forty churches. Then shouldn't the Alli-

ance be subsidizing the ethnic districts until they reach that magical mark of forty churches?

Of course, there are two sides to the financial issue. The other side is the reluctance of the Native Churches to assume fiscal responsibility. "Churches which were started under the old system—before the formation of the District—have had a hard time changing their philosophy to an indigenous one from a mission way of thinking." [68] By "mission way of thinking," what is meant is an expectation that says we (the Native Churches) are to be on the receiving end of giving. We have no giving responsibilities. People from the outside will take care of our needs. In contrast, the indigenous philosophy says, "We are responsible before God to meet the needs of our church." There is a danger when any people group looks to its denomination to continually supply its needs. It can easily assume or expect an unlimited amount of aid. Only God is this resourceful!

Often people suppose the main reason the native churches don't support a pastor is because the people are living at poverty level. It is true that many Native Americans earn below-average wages, but I do not believe this is the main reason. A couple of years ago, an Anglo lady went to be with the Lord leaving a sizable amount of money in her will to a specific Native Church. When the church received this money, the people stopped giving to the church until the money from the will was gone. I believe this shows part of the difficulty is in the way the people look at the finances of the church. If there is sufficient money to cover the needs, why give? Some have taught the responsibility of the believer to support the local church and the pastor, but we need to find ways to culturally make stewardship of our resources understood.

I have had a couple Native Americans explain to me that for their culture it is considered promoting laziness to pay a man for being the spiritual leader. He needs to work full time plus be the spiritual leader. This cultural thinking goes against biblical teaching. It needs to be addressed at every level, not just preached from the pulpit.

3. Finding, developing and keeping leaders for the Native American ministry has been a big problem from the beginning. Seeing the ineffectiveness of reaching Native Americans while working in a structure based on Western thinking has led to many leaders leaving the work and/or the Alliance. After seventy years of ministry the problem has not grown smaller. Instead it has become bigger. During the '40s and '50s, Mokahum Bible School was the hope for supplying leaders. In the '70s, this hope switched to the TEE program. For the TEE program to be successful, it needs to be owned by the people and it needs to be taught in a healthy church. When it is tried in a struggling, weak church, it is greatly limited in what it will produce as leaders. We in the Alliance need to take a long hard look at some of the difficulties we have seen in producing leaders.

First, there has been a lack of biblical accountability and applying church discipline. Or to put it another way, the lack of willingness to confront a brother or sister in Christ when we suspect doctrinal or moral error. Without accountability there is no support system to help carry us through the hard and discouraging times.

A second area that has worked against developing and keeping leaders is the area of finances. There are a couple of reasons why finances are a hindrance. Times have changed the way people look at working for God. Today it is viewed as an occupation instead of as a calling, a business instead of a ministry. This means people are not willing to work if they don't receive what they consider to be an adequate financial reward. We need to get back to the thinking of the early workers. They had a calling from God, and they were going to carry it out. They trusted God to meet their needs. They sacrificed their salaries in order to purchase land and buildings in which to meet.

We need to learn from the past. There is a need for Native American men and women who have had formal training in a Bible School. More Native Americans are earning graduate degrees. For a man to effectively pastor these people, he is going to need a graduate degree. Part of this training needs to be in the area of Native American cultures and contextualization. Yet others will find the training given by the TEE program very adequate for their ministry. We can't be emphasizing one method over the other. If the Alliance is going to meet the full cultural spectrum of Native Americans today, we need both a Bible school education at the graduate level and the TEE program.

4. An emphasis in the past twenty years has been put on reaching the Native Americans in the cities. What the workers in the District have observed is that there are many similarities between reservation works and urban works. Both struggle to support a pastor and to financially take care of facilities. Both ministries tend to develop along clan/family lines or in the urban setting, tribal lines. The size of the church on the reservation and in the urban setting are pretty much the same. An average size would be about twenty people.

Yet there are some differences. The issue of contextualization is much stronger in the cities than on the reservations. The use of objects and symbols tends to be different in the cities than on the reservations. For example, Christians who have been raised in the traditional ways of the Sioux tend to frown on Christians having eagle feathers because they understand the spiritual significance of the feathers as identification with the eagle spirit. To them it would be like Korean Christians having a statue of Buddha in their houses to say they are Korean. On the other hand some Native Americans who have been raised in the cities within the Western culture would see feathers as a symbol of being Native American, nothing more. This difference in how objects and traditions are viewed by those raised traditionally and those raised in the Western culture is growing into a watershed issue. The larger evangelical Native Community is beginning to address these issues.

Conclusion

The Christian and Missionary Alliance started to recognize the need for its Native American outreach to become indigenous in the early '50s. It made some positive steps in the direction of indiginezation. The process has to start with the right to be self-governing. The process cannot and will not be successful if we start by asking the churches to become self-supporting first! The best way to reach the Native American population in the US is through a strong, healthy indigenous church.

Back in 1975, when the Native American District was formed, there were eleven groups, two of which were organized churches. In 1997, in the Native American District, there were thirteen, of which four were organized churches. Not much progress in twenty-two years! Some works have been closed or lost. Some new ones have been started. You might look at this twenty-two-year period and say that it points to the failure of the indigenous church philosophy. But I don't believe we can accurately say this, because as I have shown in this paper, the ministry has not become indigenous. So the past twenty-two years are not twenty-two years of operating under indigenous principles. They are twenty-two years of operating under mainly a mission mentality. The work still needs to become fully indigenous. May God help us as a denomination to work together for that end.

Endnotes

[1] Anna Sontra, "Rocky Mountain District Women's Work Notes," Rocky Mountain District of The Christian and Missionary Alliance, n.d.

[2] Rev. Eugene Hall, phone conversation concerning the start of the work in Lumberton, North Carolina, summer 1997.

[3] Report of the Home Committee of the Northwestern District of The Christian and Missionary Alliance, 1945.

[4] Anna Sontra, "Rocky Mountain District Women's Work Notes."

[5] Report of the District Superintendent of the Rocky Mountain District of The Christian and Missionary Alliance, 1949.

[6] Ibid.

[7] American Indian Missions Report of the Northwestern District of The Christian and Missionary Alliance, 1948.

[8] Report of Committee on Indian Work, Rocky Mountain District Conference of The Christian and Missionary Alliance, 1947.

[9] Report of Indian Committee at the Rocky Mountain District Conference of The Christian and Missionary Alliance, 1949.

[10] American Indian Mission Report to the Northwestern District Conference, of The Christian and Missionary Alliance, 1950.

[11] American Indian Missions Report to the Northwestern District Conference of The Christian and Missionary Alliance, 1948.

[12] Keith Bailey, "Report from the Director of Indian Work Office," Rocky Mountain District Conference of The Christian and Missionary Alliance, 1950.

[13] Keith Bailey, "American Indian Missions Report," Northwestern District of the Christian and Missionary Alliance, 1950.

[14] Ibid.

[15] District Superintendent's Report of the Northwestern District of The Christian and Missionary Alliance, 1950.

[16] Keith Bailey, "American Indian Missions Report," Northwestern District Conference of The Christian and Missionary Alliance, 1951.

[17] Ibid.

[18] Ibid.

[19] Bailey, 1950.

[20] Ibid.

[21] Bailey, 1951.

[22] Ibid.

[23] Keith Bailey, "American Indian Missions Report," Northwestern District of The Christian and Missionary Alliance, 1953.

[24] Ibid.

[25] Erwin Brueckner, "Alliance Mission to the American Indians Annual Report," to the Northwestern District of The Christian and Missionary Alliance, 1954.

[26] Ibid.

[27] Rev. Eugene Hall, 1997.

[28] Fern Williams, conversation with the author concerning the history of the Alliance work with the Native Americans, summer 1997.

[29] Keith Bailey, "Alliance Mission to the American Indians Annual Report" to the Northwestern District of The Christian and Missionary Alliance, 1954, first section.

[30] "Indian Committee Report" to the Northwestern District Conference of The Christian and Missionary Alliance, 1954.

[31] Brueckner, "Alliance Mission to the American Indians Annual Report" to the Northwestern District of The Christian and Missionary Alliance, 1954.

[32] Ibid., 1955, 1956

[33] "District Superintendent's Report" to the Northwestern District Conference of The Christian and Missionary Alliance, 1957.

[34] Herman Williams, conversation with the author about the history of the Alliance with Native Americans, 1997.

[35] Leslie Pippert, "Alliance Mission to the American Indians Annual Report" to the Northwestern District Conference of The Christian and Missionary Alliance, 1958.

[36] Carl Volstad, "Alliance Mission to the American Indians Annual Report" to the Northwestern District Conference of The Christian and Missionary Alliance, 1959.

[37] "Report of the Committee on Indian Work" to the Northwestern District of The Christian and Missionary Alliance, 1961.

[38] "Report of the Assistant District Superintendent" to the Northwestern District of The Christian and Missionary Alliance, 1961.

[39] "Report of the Committee on Indian Work" to the Northwestern District Conference of The Christian and Missionary Alliance, 1962.

[40] Ibid.

[41] "Report of the Committee on Indian Work" to the Northwestern District Conference of The Christian and Missionary Alliance, 1963.

[42] "Report of the Committee on Indian Work" to the Northwestern District Conference of The Christian and Missionary Alliance, 1964.

[43] Ibid.

[44] "Report of the Assistant District Superintendent of the Northwestern District" to the District Conference of The Christian and Missionary Alliance, 1966.

[45] Richard Colenso, "Report of the Committee on Indian Work," at the District Conference in the Northwestern District of The Christian and Missionary Alliance, 1964.

[46] "Report of the District Superintendent of the Northwestern District" to the District Conference of the Northwestern District of The Christian and Missionary Alliance, 1966.

[47] "Report of the Assistant District Superintendent" to the District Conference of the Northwestern District of The Christian and Missionary Alliance, 1965.

[48] Keith Bailey, "The Annual Report of the Alliance Mission to the American Indian" at the District Conference of the Northwestern District of The Christian and Missionary Alliance, 1953.

[49] Herman Williams, interviewed by the author in Tuba City, Arizona, summer 1997.

[50] Helen Johnson, interviewed by the author at Gettysburg, South Dakota, summer 1997.

[51] Dan Wetzel, "Cover Letter to the Preliminary Report on the Relocation of Mokahum Bible School," 1975.

[52] Kenneth Doughman, "Report of Mokahum Indian Bible School" to the District Conference of the Northwestern District of The Christian and Missionary Alliance, 1970.

[53] "Report of the District Superintendent" to the District Conference of the Northwestern District of The Christian and Missionary Alliance, 1953.

[54] "Bylaws of the Alliance Indian Conference" from the District Conference of Alliance Indian District of The Christian and Missionary Alliance, Sisseton, South Dakota, 1978.

[55] Herman Williams, summer 1997.

[56] Ibid.

[57] Ibid.

[58] "Minutes from the Field Executive Committee of the Native American District" of the Christian and Missionary Alliance, Cass Lake, Minnesota, 1979.

[59] "Native American District Conference Minutes," Aberdeen, South Dakota, 1979.

[60] *Manual of The Christian and Missionary Alliance*, 1994 ed., E14-1.

[61] "Minutes from the Indian Committee" of the Native American District in The Christian and Missionary Alliance, Sisseton, South Dakota, 1978.

[62] Craig Smith, interviewed by the author, summer 1997.

[63] Steve Wood, "Report of the Administrative Assistant of the AICC," 1983.

[64] Field Executive Committee Report, September 11, 1986.

[65] "Minutes of the Native American District Conference," Phoenix, Arizona, 1984.

[66] Stephen Wood, "Quarterly Report of the Assistant to the Native American Director of the Native America District," Phoenix, Arizona, 1988.

[67] "Minutes of Native American Conference" of The Christian and Missionary Alliance, Colorado Springs, 1989.

[68] Stephen Wood, "Summary of TEE Work," 1985.

Training Missionaries
to Reach Resistant Peoples

Timothy C. Tennent

Introduction

The purpose of this article is to explore how we who are involved in the training and preparation of a new generation of missionaries can best prepare them to reach resistant peoples with the gospel of Jesus Christ. The first part of this article will make some defining observation about the expression "resistant peoples." The latter part of the article will make several strategic points which are designed to provoke reflection on some new and better ways of training missionaries who face this task. In both cases this paper is designed to be practical in its orientation.

What Is Meant by "Resistant Peoples"?

When we raise the question concerning how we can best train workers to reach "resistant peoples," we are met with an important challenge—what do we mean by the phrase "resistant peoples"? While the term is widely used in our classrooms, the literature and in the local church, it is an insufficient phrase for those of us involved in strategic planning—insufficient because it is too vague and too broad to say anything meaningful at the strategic planning level.

For example, one can quickly note that there are at least four categories of resistant peoples which make up the unreached world, with an accompanying host of variations and combinations on each of the themes.

First, there are those groups which are *culturally resistant*. Recall, for example, how D. Hesselgrave has reminded us of Nietzche's and Ruth Benedict's analysis of certain societies which may be termed "Apollonian" societies, antagonistic to change, as opposed to "Dionysian" cultures, receptive to change.[1] It is a simple rubric underlying an important point. Namely, some societies resist change simply because all change, indeed, *any* change is perceived to be bad. The truth claims of the gospel cannot easily undermine a pre-existing cultural bias against accepting any new beliefs or practices. We can restate the gospel in a dozen different ways; it still doesn't matter, because it represents change.

Second, there are those groups which may be called theologically resistant. These groups, ranging from Mormons to Muslims, have been predisposed to reject certain Christian doctrines out of hand because of their own theological self-understanding. Their beliefs have been shaped by an explicit rejection of certain particulars of Christian theology, whether real or perceived, genuine or caricatured. "Allah has no partners," claims the Muslim; to affirm the Sonship and Deity of Jesus Christ represents a fundamental theological impossibility.[2] We must be prepared to discuss detailed theological questions and issues regarding the Deity and Sonship of Jesus Christ.

Third, there are those groups which are *nationalistically or ethnically resistant*. Such a group's identity, not theologically, but ethnically, involves a rejection of another group, including their beliefs. The Tiv in middle-belt Nigeria, for example, resisted Islam not because of its theological content, the insufficiency of its truth claims or the weakness of its worldview, but because the dominating Hausa of the upper-belt were Muslim. Precisely because the Hausa were fiercely committed to Islam and in those trappings victimized them, that meant that the Tiv would be predisposed to resist Islam. Likewise, there are groups who identify Christianity with Westernization or with colonialism or some other alien factor which causes the group to reject Christianity.

Many of the nineteenth-century Hindu revival groups such as the Arya Samaj and Brahmo Samaj rallied around a revitalized

Hinduism because it was a way of reasserting traditional Indianness in a context dominated by British colonialism. My Ph.D. dissertation focused on the Bengali theologian Brahmabandhav Upadhyay. Before he came to Christ he was convinced that being a Christian meant having to wear pants, eat meat and drink alcohol. Once he came to Christ he spent the rest of his life seeking to demonstrate that being a Christian was not tantamount to renouncing his Indian heritage and culture.

Finally, there are resistant groups which are *politically resistant*. Included here are those which are behind political walls where traditional missionary work is not permited, and since their confines are also frequently lacking a viable witnessing church, we assume that they are resistant. In fact, many have never had the opportunity to even hear or respond to the gospel, and therefore our assessment that they are resistant may be premature. How do you compare the 23 million Koreans who have not heard the gospel because of the political realities in North Korea with the Malayalam speaking Mappillas off the coast of Southwest India who have repeatedly rejected the gospel and remain fiercely Islamic?[3] There is a significant strategic difference in our approach to such groups.

The world encompasses a wide variety of reasons for resistance or perceived resistance: cultural, theological, national and political, among others, as well as combinations of these. Each reason requires different kinds of strategies if we are to be effective in the task of training those God has given to us. Therefore, we must do a much better job articulating what we mean by "resistant peoples."

With these observations in mind, let us now turn to some strategic reflections.

Some Strategic Reflections

At Toccoa Falls College we are currently seeking to equip around 140 mission majors, many of whom are committed to reaching resistant peoples in several of the above categories. I would like to highlight six principles which are helping to guide our training process.

First, without sacrificing the time spent grounding our students in the biblical message, *we must become more receptor-oriented in our training.* That is, we must help our students not only to understand the gospel message, but to understand it in light of the beliefs, worldviews, perceptions and challenges of those on the receiving end. This means an increased emphasis on anthropology, world religions, cross-cultural communication and cross-cultural theologizing. Put quite plainly, it is not unusual for people groups in the 10-40 Window to ask a whole range of new questions which our Western theologizing has not prepared us to answer.

I have had the privilege for several years of teaching the main academic year here in the United States and then teaching in India each summer. Offering many of the same courses on two different continents has been a very constructive way to observe how theology is formulated in two different cultures. What has struck me is that my Indian students persistently ask their own set of questions. Consequently, I have been singularly impressed with the need to do a better job in formulating theology cross-culturally.[4]

Our program at Toccoa Falls College is rooted in an anthropology core of four courses in sequence as well as courses which acquaint students in the beliefs of the target people groups.[5] We offer courses in belief systems, world religions and even individual courses in Islam, Hinduism and Buddhism. This not only gives us sufficient time to explore the beliefs of the receptor groups, but also to examine specific strategies currently being used to reach them. We have become far more intentional in preparing our students to understand the beliefs, worldviews, thinking processes, cultures, etc., of the target group. This emphasis has helped us in the task of contextualization as well as in the task of de-contextualization, i.e., learning to separate the Christian gospel from elements in our own culture which we have unwittingly united with the *kerygma*, the gospel core.

Second, we as missiologists need to increase our discussions about bolder forms of contextualization. Whether we are talking about Jesus Mosques in Bangladesh for Islamic converts, Christian

Sannyasins in India for former Hindus or Soka Gakkai-styled lay discussion and discipleship groups in Japan to win and grow Buddhist converts, new ideas are being promoted today in ways we haven't seen on this scale. The last few issues of *Mission Frontiers* have been highlighting this development. I was pleased to read the report in the August 1997 issue of the Southern Baptists' *Commission* magazine and later reprinted in *Mission Frontiers* about the Jesus Mosques and the work in Benin. This is, of course, only one part of a larger movement within some mission circles to experiment with bolder forms of contextualization.

One of the comments made in the *Missions Frontiers* article by those opposed to Jesus' Mosques was the following statement: "Muslim forms cannot be divorced from their meanings."[6] That has to be one of the most theologically-loaded phrases I've read in some time. If that statement is true, then it reverberates outward affecting all of our missiological strategy. If it is not, we still have to seriously discuss how Islamic or Hindu or Buddhist forms might be legitimately redirected toward Christian ends. We desperately need far more interaction about the pros and cons of using and/or redirecting and/or replacing non-Christian religious forms with Christian ones.

Third, we must train our students to be trainers and equip them to be equippers. Three of the four types of resistance outlined earlier all demand an increased emphasis on our promoting "in culture" changes, rather than using external agents of change from outside the culture such as is sometimes promoted overtly or inadvertently in traditional Western missionary outreach. Take for example an Apollonian culture which is against change for change's sake; or a culture proud of its own ethnic heritage and suspicious of a Westerner; or a culture with political restrictions which make long term residency of Western missionaries illegal. In all three of these cases, the answer is found in an increased emphasis on the non-Western missionary—someone who is either a member of the target culture or a near culture member.

Certainly one of the most dramatic changes in the twentieth

century has been the emergence of third-world missions. In India, for example, since the early '70s when India ceased issuing new visas for Western missionaries, the missionary force began a rapid decline from thousands down to just a few hundred. Fortunately, for every Western missionary who left India, God has raised up at least two national Indian workers who are crossing cultural boundaries with the gospel. It would be foolish for a Western organization today to target India without networking with indigenous believers. It would be foolish for a Western organization to target Muslims in Nigeria, for example, without taking into account the growth of new Christians among the people groups in middle-belt Nigeria.

Networking with national believers also helps to prevent the notion that we have been set apart as the guardians of global orthodoxy. Are we really in a position, for example, to decide which African Independent Churches (AICs) are "in" and which ones are "out" based on *our* understanding of *their* orthodoxy? Western formulations of theology may not always be entirely applicable in their contexts. Sometimes we are simply unable to "hear" their orthodoxy because it is not being expressed in the familiar strains and forms of our own theological traditions.

I have been involved for the last ten years in a church-planting ministry in northern India which trains Indians from southern India to plant churches in the north.[7] Southern Indians are culturally distant from Nothern Indians, but they are still far more effective and culturally close than a missionary from the West. I applaud several new ministries such as the International Institute of Christian Studies who have committed themselves and their resources not to sending missionaries to do missions per se, but to sending missionaries to train and equip national believers to more effectively carry out their God-given task of reaching the unreached people groups in their country for Christ. We need to acquaint our students with these kind of ministries, both in the classroom and in their field internships.

Networking with third-world missions is not the first step in relinquishing our role in global evangelism. On the contrary, every church on every continent should be both a sending and a receiving church. We have gifts which the global Church needs. Likewise, we need the insights and experiences of our brothers and sisters around the world to help in our own appreciation of the full grandeur of the Church of Jesus Christ.

Fourth, we must continue to be vigilant in recognizing the vital link between missiology and theology. Solid, biblical theology should lie at the heart of our missiological task. I see theological challenges both from without and within which deserve our attention.

First, as noted earlier, we face unique theological challenges from without. We must help our students to understand the difference, for example, between the theological challenges which face us in an Islamic context versus the theological challenges which face us in a Hindu context. We must give our students the theological preparation to face new questions which often are not raised, or are not raised in the same way, in our normal biblical and theological courses. In our courses on Islam and Hinduism respectively, a great deal of time is spent dealing with the theological issues and challenges which arise out of these unique contexts.

Second, we face theological challenges from within. We must increase our vigilance in defending historic doctrines such as the uniqueness of Christ, the importance of personal response and the centrality of the Great Commission in the Church's mission among our own. It takes spiritual conviction to give your life to reaching resistant peoples. Granted, many of our students want to go and "do" missions for a summer here or have a cross-cultural experience there, but we need people prepared to commit their lives to full-time mission work.

The problem is, the very basis for missions which provides the motivation for students is being eroded even within evangelicalism. The most blatant example is the problem of creeping inclusivism which continues to seep into the consciousness of the postmodern evangelical community. I want to say clearly that, from my understanding of Scripture, any theology, whether it comes from Catholic or Protestant circles, which says that

Christ's death is central, but a conscious response to the name of Jesus is not, undermines the very foundation of the Great Commission and is in direct violation of Acts 4:12 and Romans 10:13-15. To say that Jesus' death is ontologically essential but not epistemologically necessary is nothing but a thinly veiled theological construct which repeats the old problem of separating the Jesus of history from the Christ of faith. Faith must be explicitly in the historical, objective work of God in Jesus Christ, not merely a subjective experience of "faith" which is not necessarily or cognitively related to Jesus Christ. Our evangelical students coming to us in the last several years are already predisposed towards inclusivism. We can no longer assume that our students share our theological convictions. This has led us to be more intentional in the theological preparation of those who are considering a career in cross-cultural work.

Fifth, we must continue to encourage the training of Christian tentmakers. If ninety percent of the unreached people groups are in the 10-40 Window and the vast majority of the political countries within the 10-40 Window prohibit traditional missionary access, then it is only logical that a much higher percentage of our resources should be utilized to equip and to provide the missionary structures so that our students can enter restricted access countries as professionals, not as traditional missionaries. Accordingly, our program at Toccoa Falls has two main tracks with several different majors under each track. We have a missiology track which trains and equips our students for traditional missionary access endeavors, especially church planting, which is paramount to any vital missionary program.

But we also have a second track called Cross-Cultural Studies. The very name of the degree diffuses possible problems for our students entering sensitive countries. Within the track we have two majors: medical professionals, for those training to be doctors or nurses; and TESOL, Teaching English to Speakers of Other Languages. Approximately one-third of our majors in the School of World Missions at Toccoa Falls College are preparing to be English-language professionals. In addition to our normal anthropological and missiological training and the required hours in Bible and theology, they will take Introduction to TESOL, Methods and Materials of TESOL, TESOL Practicum and Communicating Values through TESOL. The result is that a number of our graduates are landing jobs to teach English in China, Japan, Mongolia and Kazakhstan—all countries within the 10-40 Window. Tentmakers have the advantage of being able to get to the field quicker and to get into the 10-40 Window with long-term visas. Also, they require far less resources from the sending church since they are all either fully or partially self-supporting.

Sixth, we need to integrate the strategic role of prayer and personal devotion into our overall professional training. We no longer have the luxury of assuming that our students have solid personal lives with deep relationships with Christ who only need the professional skills and tools to get the job done. Our students need to be taught and given models of prayer and personal devotion to God. Spiritual formation is as important as professional formation. The recent "Praying through the Window III" which culminated in the Praying Through the Window daily during the month of October 1997 has been one of the best initiatives in recent years to help our students in this area. Spiritual strongholds operative in the 10-40 Window do not collapse because we have applied the right technique, but yield, in part, because our efforts have been bathed in prayer and our dependence is upon the Lord Jesus Christ to go before us. We begin classes by praying for an unreached group and set aside regular prayer times when we as the faculty can get before God with our students and pray for unreached people groups. This not only gives our teaching more credibility, but it models the most important part of our task as missionaries.

In conclusion, besides challenging us to rethink what is meant by the expression "resistant peoples," I have attempted to point out some practical ways which might help us in our common calling to equip a new generation of missionaries to complete the Great Commission. May the new rally cry, *"all peoples—nothing less,"* be increasingly true as we seek to finish the task given to us by our Lord Jesus Christ.

Endnotes

1 D. Hesselgrave, *Communicating Christ Cross-Culturally*, 2nd ed. (Grand Rapids, MI: Zondervan, 1991), 591.

2 See, for example, such passages in the Qu'ran as 2:116, 117; 10:68; 17:111; 51:51.

3 Joshua Project 2000, *Unreached Peoples List*, 4, 8.

4 Two of the most helpful books in this area are Lamin Sanneh, *Translating the Message: The Missionary Impact on Culture* (Maryknoll, NY: Orbis, 1989) and Lamin Sanneh, *Encountering the West: Christianity and the Global Cultural Process* (Maryknoll, NY: Orbis, 1993). Books such as Eugene Nida and William Reyburn, *Meaning Across Cultures* (Maryknoll, NY: Orbis, 1981) and Dean Gilliland, *The Word Among Us* (Waco, TX: Word, 1989) provide excellent demonstration of the need for a contextualized theology. Much of the work of such theologies is still quite young.

5 We offer the following anthropology core: Cultural Anthropology, Applied Anthropology, Ethnography, Religious Belief Systems.

6 *Mission Frontiers Bulletin* (July-October 1997): 19. The statement was made by Warren Chastain of the Zwemer Institute of Muslim Studies. The article is a reprint from the August 1997 issue of the *Commission*, a magazine of the International Mission Board, Southern Baptist Convention.

7 The Indian church-planting organization is Bharat Susamachar Samiti and is primarily known for its theological training institute in Dehra Dun, U.P., called the Luther W. New, Jr. Theological College, or NTC.

Premillennialism and
the Alliance Distinctives

Joel Van Hoogen

What relevancy does premillennialism hold for modern evangelicalism? In particular, how relevant is it in giving focus and direction to The Christian and Missionary Alliance? What bearing does premillennialism have on Alliance distinctives? Is ownership of this doctrine really that essential to the future effectiveness of the ministry of the Alliance? In seeking to give answer to these questions it would be wise to set forward some of the distinctives within the Alliance that have uniquely shaped it, distinctives it would affirm as essential components for the future. Five such distinctives are suggested for consideration:

First, The Christian and Missionary Alliance is a missionary denomination. It exists as a denomination primarily to reach the world for Christ. It is foremost an alliance of Christian and missionary churches. It was such an alliance long before it was ever a denomination.

Second, the Alliance has a deeper life message with a strong emphasis on the life of Christ within the believer. There is an expectation of holiness in the child of God because of the wonderful mystery revealed which makes this possible. The mystery is that by faith through death to self, the life of Christ is imparted with power to God's children so that they may live whole and holy lives.

Third, the Alliance has offered to evangelicalism a unique insight into Christology. This is possibly its most significantly distinct contribution to the modern-day Church. This Christology focuses upon the centrality of Christ in everything. Christ is more than the Giver, He is the Gift. With Him the Christian has everything, for in Him are all things. Without Him, one has nothing. The Alliance does say that Jesus is Savior, but would add that He is Salvation. It would affirm that Jesus is Sanctifier, but would add that He is Sanctification. He is Healer, and yet He is more. It is His life, He Himself, that brings health. Over and over it may be emphasized that Jesus is central and all in all. This is the meaning of the fourfold gospel.

Fourth, the Alliance holds to the infallible Word of God. This is not a unique distinctive of the Alliance, but it certainly is a distinctive emphasis which it would affirm as an essential component for its future.

Fifth, the Alliance has a high view of the transcendent integrity of God. This too is not a distinctive unique to The Christian and Missionary Alliance, but it is an emphasis that has found a vital expression in its folds. Dr. A.W. Tozer, for one, was used wonderfully of God to encourage and champion this high and lofty focus upon God in the churches of the Alliance.

As the premillennial position of the Alliance is considered, it should be weighed in the light of these five distinctives. Conversely, these five distinctives can be understood more fully in the light of this position on premillennial doctrine. To develop this understanding, the following outline will be followed:

1. Summary of the three basic positions on the millennium.
2. The Statement of Faith of The Christian and Missionary Alliance and the corresponding views of Dr. A.B. Simpson, its founder.
3. The historical development of millennialism.
4. Interpretations of Revelation 20:1-6.
5. The relevance of premillennialism for the future of The Christian and Missionary Alliance.

1. Summary of the Three Basic Millennial Positions

It is not possible without some significant generalizing to discuss the various eschatological positions on the millennium. There is a wide range of interpretive variance in each of the three positions outlined.

Postmillennialism

Postmillennialism is a theological position that affirms the second coming of Jesus Christ at the end of the millennial period.

The millennium is to be a literal period of 1,000 years of peace and righteousness in the age preceding the return of Jesus Christ. During this time the gospel will be universally preached and broadly received. Postmillennialists generally hold to a spiritual interpretation which states, "the kingdom of God is a state of society in which the will of God is done in the hearts of 'born again' believers."[1] Thus the kingdom will grow until the world is Christianized. At the end of the millennium an outbreak of wickedness will occur, identified as the Great Tribulation. Then Christ shall return, bringing a general resurrection of the dead and ushering in the eternal state with a new heaven and earth.

Amillennialism

Amillennialism is a theological position which affirms the second coming of Christ after a millennial period. Amillennialists are not truly "a" (no) "millennial," since they do believe in a spiritualized millennium. The 1,000 years are to be understood as figurative of the completed present period from the resurrection of Christ to His second coming. Christ's reign in this millennium is spiritual in the lives of those newborn and occurs simultaneously as this evil age progresses becoming worse and worse. At the same time it is acknowledged that Satan is, in this time, uniquely bound so that he may not deceive the nations, guaranteeing that some from every tribe and tongue will believe in Christ. This age will end in the climax of a great tribulation, after which Christ shall return and usher in the eternal state with a new heaven and earth.

Premillennialism

Premillennialism is the belief that Christ's second coming precedes His earthly rule and the visible implementation of His kingdom of peace and righteousness. He shall personally reign upon the earth with His saints.

The 1,000 years will be literal. Christ's reign upon the earth will be literal. Satan will be bound so that he cannot promote evil in man's fallen nature and in the social order. During this time God will bring into one both the natural and the spiritual Israel and provide the literal fulfillment of His promises to Abraham, Isaac, Jacob and their seed. This age will commence after the Great Tribulation and will conclude with one final outbreak of evil, at which point Christ will put down all evil and usher in the eternal state with a new heaven and earth.

2. The Statement of Faith of the Alliance and the Corresponding Views of Dr. A.B. Simpson

Article 11 of the statement of faith of the Alliance reads, "The second coming of the Lord Jesus Christ is imminent and will be personal, visible, and premillennial. This is the believer's blessed hope and is a vital truth which is an incentive to holy living and faithful service."

As the Alliance moved toward a more formal denominational structure, they adopted a formal statement of faith at their annual Council in 1965, which was derived from long-held beliefs within the movement. As such there was little debate and disagreement on the positions brought forward. In the discussion from the floor on Article 11 the term "imminent" was opposed by a small contingent, but it was defeated soundly. A few also voiced opposition to the term "premillennial." They were, according to Dr. Keith Bailey, a witness to the debate, "stomped" by the affirmative voters. Such a unified embrace of this doctrine was to be expected, when the strong premillennial sentiment of the founder of the Alliance is taken into consideration.

Any casual reading of the poetry of Dr. Simpson will reveal a common theme celebrating the premillennial return of Christ.

In A.B. Simpson's book, *The Coming One*, his view of the millennium and his perspective on the importance of the doctrine in the life of the Church are stated. Dr. Simpson states the belief that Christ is yet to come to earth to complete His glorious redemptive plan. He rejected any notion that the promises regarding Christ's millennial coming were fulfilled in the death of the saints, the destruction of Jerusalem, a spiritual indwelling or in any spiritual application through the Church. He spoke against a spiritualizing interpretation of Old Testament prophetic passages. He spoke against the blotting out of the literal Israel from God's future plans. He wrote, "There is a double thread running through the warp and woof of ancient prophecy. There is the crimson line of the cross, but there is the golden thread of the coming glory. . . . It was necessary that He should fulfill the vision of the cross and it is just as necessary that He shall fulfill the vision of the King." [2]

The rejection of a material, terrestrial millennium for a higher spiritual one of heart or heaven (such as amillennialism may design) was to Dr. Simpson compatible with spiritualizing the creation account or the liberalizing of Jesus into an idea with no historical reality. "Such a rejection," he wrote, "takes out of God's Book all reality and makes everything merely a dream as vague as the fooleries of Christian Science. Thank God He is real and we are real and Christ is real and the coming glory is real." [3]

With similar vibrato, Dr. Simpson reacted against the more commonly held postmillennial views of the day, calling them counterfeit millenniums:

> Man has tried to make his own millennium. Poetry has dreamed of it, and degraded it into a sensuous paradise. Patriots and optimists have drawn the vision of a golden age of liberty, equality, peace, and plenty, and have seen only anarchy, license, and misery arise at the touch of their deceptive wand. Moralists have toiled for purity, temperance, and virtue, and dreamed of a day when social reform will have blotted out the last plague spot from

our cities, only to see wickedness, crime, and the curse of alcohol, and woman's shame increase with increasing civilization. And Christian reformers have expected a spiritual millennium, in which the Gospel shall cover the myriad populations of earth, and make every land a holy, happy paradise of love and purity; but alas! the lands that are the most evangelized are sometimes the farthest from millennial piety or purity; and were all the world to reach tomorrow the condition to which Christian lands have attained in the three centuries since the Reformation, earth would still be a sight to break the heart of Him who died for us. Nay, God has something better for His weary, hungry children than any of man's counterfeit millenniums.[4]

3. The Historical Development of Millennialism

It should be noted that the doctrinal thought of Dr. A.B. Simpson—and The Christian and Missionary Alliance, for that matter—are products of their times. The Alliance was born during a period of time when premillennial thought and its attendant biblicism were being renewed in church history. To help contextualize the premillennial thought of Dr. Simpson's day, the historical flow of millennial thought from the apostles down to the present follows.

The Premillennial Early Church

The observation shared by the vast majority of historians is that the early Church was premillennial. George N.H. Peters chronicles in proposition 72 of his voluminous work, *The Theocratic Kingdom*, a compelling historical argument demonstrating that the premillennial doctrine of the kingdom, as preached by the apostles, was taught by the early churches.[5]

The following is a sampling of a few of the church and secular historians whose studies have concurred with George N.H. Peters' basic proposition: Edward Gibbon, author of the classic work, *The History of the Decline and Fall of the Roman Empire;* J.C.I. Gieseler, Professor of Theology and highly acclaimed church historian in his day, who himself was not a premillennialist; Henry Sheldon, Professor of Historical Theology at Boston University; Philip Schaff, prominent German reformed theologian, church historian and author of the monumental eight volume, *History of the Christian Church*; Adolf Harnack, Lutheran theologian and church historian; Will Durant, author of the multi-volume work, *The Story of Civilization*; Paul Boyer, Professor of History at the University of Wisconsin, Madison, and author of *When Time Shall Be No More: Prophecy Belief in Modern American Culture.*

Many of the early Church Fathers revealed a premillennial indoctrination. *The Epistle of Barnabas* (c. A.D. 70) was written only a little after the martyrdom of the apostle Paul. On the creation week, it says:

> Consider what this signifies, He finished them in six days. The meaning of it is this; that in six thousand years the Lord God will bring all things to an end. For with Him one day is as a thousand years. . . . [T]herefore . . . in six days (i.e., 6,000 years) shall all things be accomplished. . . . [W]hen His Son shall come and abolish the wicked one, and judge the ungodly; and shall change the sun, and moon and stars; then He shall gloriously rest on that 'seventh day,' i.e., millennium.[6]

Papias (c. A.D. 60-130) was reputed to have been taught by John the apostle. Fanciful images of a millennial period are attributed to him.

Justin Martyr (A.D. 100-165) wrote, "I and others who are right-minded Christians on all points, are assured that there will be a resurrection of the dead and a thousand years in Jerusalem, which will then be built, adorned, and enlarged, as the prophets Ezekiel and Isaiah and others declare."[7] Martyr's clear premillennialism prompted Harnack to observe, "That a philosopher like Justin, with a bias towards an Hellenic construction of the Christian religion, should nevertheless have accepted its chiliastic elements is the strongest proof that these enthusiastic expectations were inseparably bound up with the Christian faith down to the middle of the second century."[8]

Irenaeus (A.D. 140-203) was the disciple of Polycarp, the disciple of John the apostle. He affirmed the millennium and two distinct resurrections.

Tertullian (A.D. 170-220) believed in the primacy of the literal sense of Scripture and that a literal millennium would follow the resurrection of the dead. He went deeply into the book of Daniel and taught that Daniel 9:24-27 predicted both the time of Christ's birth and death. He saw the millennium as an interim kingdom before the final translation of the saints into heaven. Tertullian fascinatingly observed, "At His last coming He will favor with His acceptance and blessing the circumcision also, even the race of Abraham, which by and by is to acknowledge Him."[9]

Hippolytus (A.D. 170-236) was a presbyter of the church of Rome. He set out the most complete source of the customs of the ante-Nicene church in his *Commentary on the Book of Daniel*, a premillennial eschatology.

Nephos of Egypt (first half of the third century) wrote a tract entitled *Against the Allegorist* in which he defended the literal, traditional interpretation of the millenarian promises in Revelation 20 and 21.[10]

Sextus Julius Africanus (died A.D. 240) was a friend of the anti-millennialist Origen; in spite of this, he ". . . adopted the familiar apocalyptic notion of a "world week" of seven thousand years. . . . According to the usual form of this scheme, history will come to an end six thousand years after creation and will usher in a 'Sabbath' of a thousand years."[11]

Methodius (died A.D. 311) spoke of two resurrections and the seventh millennium of the creation.

Victorinus (died A.D. 304) held to two distinct resurrections as taken from Revelation 20, separated by 1,000 years. He expresses the seventh day as an eschatological image of the millennium.

Lactantius (died after 317 A.D.) was a confessor to Constantine. He was premillennarian and also interpreted the three-

and-one-half years of the last half of the tribulation to be a three-and-one-half year reign of terror by a Syrian king, the real Anti-Christ who will be defeated prior to the millennium by the Great King from heaven, who will then set up 1,000-year reign with the just, over the remnants of earth. During this time, the "Prince of Demons" will be chained in prison and freed at the end to lead an unsuccessful assault against God's people. God will then bring about a total transformation of this natural order. The second resurrection will then take place in which the unbelieving dead will rise to eternal punishment.[12]

Peters concluded that the premillennial return of Christ and subsequent kingdom rule was taught by the early disciples and received by the young Church and that amillennial teaching was not clearly evidenced in Church history until the time of Augustine.

Development of Amillennialism

Amillennialism first appeared in the negative sense with no positive proposition regarding the millennium. Thus, the first expressions of amillennialism were a reaction against the gross sensual extremes that characterized some expressions of the dominant literal view of the millennium. It was also trying to put distance between the Christian doctrine of the end times and what was considered Jewish sensualism.

Origen (A.D. 185-253) was the most prominent of the negative amillennialists. It was he who popularized the allegorical method of biblical interpretation which provided a means by which Greek philosophical thought could be wed to Old and New Testament passages. With this view he maintained that there were three levels of interpretation for every passage of Scripture: the literal, the moral and the allegorical. He affirmed that the literal interpretation was not essentially the correct one. Such a hermeneutic enabled him to distance himself from the literal and "sensual" sense found in much of the prophetic passages of Scripture.

A positive amillennialism did not appear until the writings of Augustine (A.D. 354-430). Augustine was the chief architect of

Catholic theology up to the time of Thomas Aquinas. His amillennial scheme is still the foundational thought behind Catholic and Reformed eschatology and millenarianism to this day. So strongly were his views adopted that church authorities went so far as to expurgate from the works of Irenaeus and Victorinus all millennial taint.[13]

Augustine was highly influenced by the Neoplatonism of Plotinus (A.D. 205-270) and the allegorical method of Philo, which Origen developed for Christian thought. This influence was profoundly dualistic. "Plato believed that the ultimate goal of a human being was to arrive at a disembodied state of pure spirit. . . . The material, and especially the body . . . was looked upon as evil and to be loathed."[14]

This dualism is seen in Augustine's writings on the afterlife and influenced his development of purgatory as a place to " . . . cleanse them from the remnants that are owing to this cement of flesh."[15]

The influence of Platonic thought is also revealed in the expressive monastic forms of Augustine's day, forms that he, in some degree, followed. Refusing to marry his common-law wife and the mother of his son, he became a celibate monk, with a monastic order following after his example.

This dualism ultimately resulted in Augustine's development of a new concept of the kingdom and the millennium. It is important when considering the history of this doctrine to note that Augustine's belief in a spiritual millennium was not the recovering of an old truth neglected, but the establishment of a new scheme, not advanced by anyone before him. Historian Christopher Dawson well observes that Augustine is "entirely alienated from the realistic literalism of the old apocalyptic tradition."[16]

As A.E. Pinell lucidly demonstrated, Augustine never attempted to refute millennialism but simply ignored it on the grounds that its materialism was unseemly. Augustine states:

> This opinion would not be objectionable, if it were believed that the joys of the saints in that Sabbath should

be spiritual only, and consequent on the presence of God. But as he asserts that those who then rise again shall enjoy the leisure of immoderate carnal banquets, famished with an amount of meat and drink such as not only to shock the feeling of the temperate, but even to surpass the measure of credulity itself, such assertions can be believed only by the carnal. They who do believe them are called by the spiritual "Chiliasts" which literally may be millenarians.[17]

Pinell gives further light on this prejudice Augustine had against millennialism by noting:

As Platonistically conditioned as he was and given his monastic mentality, it was understandable that Augustine should have reacted as he did to the millennialism of his day. His basic aversion to thinking of any future rest for the saints, as including any kind of material enjoyments, showed heavily in the reason he gave for rejecting millennialism. He said he could believe in millennialism, if it only stated that "the joys of saints in the Sabbath shall be spiritual." Otherwise, he said, "this opinion would not be objectionable." That is, to please him, an eschatological system had to be free of references to future material enjoyments. Not finding in millennialism the pure spiritual system he sought from the Christian writings of past history or from anything else, the only recourse he had left was his large and resourceful intellect.[18]

It should be noted that with the rise of Constantine and the graduation of Christianity to the official religion of the Roman Empire, there was little need to perpetuate a millennial doctrine of hope for the end of all human government upon the earth and the ushering in of a distinctly divine one. It should also be noted that from this time forward, up through the reformation period, until the early nineteenth century, the Church

51

was wedded to the leadership of, or allegiance to, earthly powers and rulers. Each of the three main Protestant traditions of the sixteenth century—Lutheranism, Calvinism and Anglicanism—had the support of the state, even as they continued in the same Constantinian (amillennial) approach to theology.[19] It is noteworthy then that with the dawning of the nineteenth century and the increasing separation of church and state, there was also a significant shift in church doctrine towards premillennial thought.

It can be said in review that Origin's attempts to allegorize, Augustine's dualistic Platonism[20] and Constantine's Christianization of human government effectively killed a vigilant spirit of defense for and development of premillennial theology. Amillennialism was not the primary historical testimony of the Church; rather, it was premillennialism that expressed the hopes of the early Church. Amillennialism did not rise out of a rediscovery of biblical truth, but out of reaction to a "Jewish sensualism" that was incompatible with the "Hellenistic dualism" of the day. Amillennialism was born out of the convergence of spiritualizing interpretation, dualistic philosophy that disparaged the physical, and realized social triumphalism. These three are generally recognized in evangelical thought as negative developments in the Church.

Yet, in spite of this suspicious genesis, today's amillennialists are satisfied to identify their position and, in particular, their reading of Revelation 20:1-6, as defensible through their allegiance to the teaching of Augustine. Anthony Hoekema, for example, states in defense of an amillennial interpretation, "The amillennial understanding of Revelation 20:1-6 as describing the reigning souls of deceased believers with Christ in heaven has had good standing in the church since the days of Augustine."[21]

Development of Postmillennialism

Postmillennialism appeared on the historical scene in the seventeenth century with the Age of Enlightenment. Augustine's anti-materialism was increasingly incompatible with a budding age of science and a focus upon a material universe. Literal measurements and calculations conflicted with the allegorical method of interpreting nature and God's Word.

With Daniel Whitby (1683-1726), a Unitarian, postmillennialism was introduced. Eventually there came about two kinds of postmillennialism. One was liberal and secular, with adherents like John Locke and Thomas Paine, and later liberals such as Shirley Jackson Case, author of *Christianizing the Social Order*. Over time there appeared many other books trumpeting the social triumph of Christianity. The other was a conservative postmillennialism represented in a chain of succession by Jonathan Edwards, Charles Hodge, B.B. Warfield and Loraine Boettner. The succession of two world wars dealt a death blow to the optimism of postmillennialism. Today the new Reconstructionism has arisen, which makes a curious blend of the two, at times militantly combining a conservative view of Scripture and the gospel with the law and its social demands and political mandates.

The Renewal of the Premillennial Doctrine

One should be aware that there is not a century from the time of the early Church where there is not some record of premillennial teaching and thought. Paul Boyer's book, *When Time Shall Be No More*, demonstrates that even during the Middle Ages the religion of the populace had strong material, premillennial hopes.[22] *The Evangelical Dictionary of Theology* confirms this point, stating that the allegorical interpretation of Augustine became the official doctrine of the Church during the medieval period. In defiance of the main teaching of the Church, however, the earlier apocalyptic premillennialism continued to be held by certain counterculture groups.[23]

Long before John Darby (1800-1882) was sketching his first dispensational charts, Joachim of Fiore (1135-1202) had sketched his three ages of law, grace and the Spirit, and was publishing his *Book of Figures* charting out these ages. Out of an inductive study of the book of Revelation he concluded that the chiliasts were right.[24]

John Wycliffe and John Hus, morning stars of the Reformation, were avowed millennialists. Premillennialists in the Reformation period also existed with more and more frequency, e.g., Joseph Mede, Isaac Watts, Hugh Latimer and Puritan John Bunyan, all argued for the literal interpretation of all the prophetic passages of Scripture. Bunyan, for example, wrote on Zechariah 14:4, "His feet shall stand in that day upon the Mount of Olives," arguing against the spiritualizers of God's Word. He says, "This is the day of His second coming," and then asks, "Where is the Mount of Olives? Not within thee! But that which is without Jerusalem." On the millennium, Bunyan further writes:

> God's blessing the Sabbath day, and resting on it from all His works, was a type of that glorious rest that saints shall have when the six days of this world are totally ended. . . . This day is called a great day . . . which shall end in the eternal judgment of the world. God hath held this forth by several other shadows, such as the Sabbath of weeks, the Sabbath of years, and the great Jubilee. . . . In the seventh thousand years of the world will be that Sabbath when Christ shall set up His kingdom on earth: according to that which is written, "They lived and reigned with Christ a thousand years."[25]

David Larsen in his book *Jews, Gentiles and the Church* makes note that Martin Bucer, successor to Zwingli, and Theodore Beza, Calvin's successor, started a small but growing trend returning to chiliasm.[26] Robert Baillie in 1645 claimed that most of the divines in London were chiliasts. By 1649 Grotius had counted eighty books published in England expounding the millennium.[27] Larsen also demonstrates a growing trend among theologians, church leaders and political leaders, such as Oliver Cromwell, to reevaluate the role of Israel in the plans of God. There was an ever-increasing embrace of the thought that Israel would have a part in the glorious plans of God and that Old Testament prophecy contained not only the glory of the New

Testament Church but a literal promise for the glory of Israel. Among those who held to an eschatological belief in the restoration of Israel were such Puritans as John Cotton, Thomas Shepherd, John Eliot, the American Mathers and John Owen.

Owen wrote, "The Jews shall be gathered from all parts of the earth where they are now scattered, and brought home into their 'homeland' before the 'end of all things' prophesied by St. Peter can occur."[28] It would be stretching it to say that these individuals were premillennialists. What would be a safe statement is that such a growing sentiment added to the ultimate climate in which premillennialism was widely embraced.

The new rise of premillennial thought, though strongly initiated by John Darby, was not the sole domain of one version of dispensational thought. There were those like Anglican Bishop of Liverpool, John Charles Ryle, who wrote the *Premillennial Creed*, and those who would now likely be called progressive dispensationalists, such as George N.H. Peters, author of the three-volume *The Theocratic Kingdom*; Nathaniel West, author of *One Thousand Years in Both Testaments*; and W.C. Stevens, a teacher at Nyack College and author of *Revelation, the Crown Jewel of Biblical Prophecy*.

According to secular historian Boyer,

> Dispensationalism arrived at a time of mounting evangelical concern over challenges to the Bible's divinely inspired status by liberal theologians in the United States and by historical-critical scholars in Germany. The formation of the Evangelical Alliance in England in 1846 and of an American branch in 1867 signaled the rising uneasiness. At the founding convention in London, the eight hundred delegates adopted a creedal statement explicitly affirming the Bible's inspiration and authority. Many embattled evangelicals thus welcomed Darby's strong emphasis on Biblical authority and his literal reading of the prophetic texts.[29]

The dispensational premillennial movement corresponded to,

and further encouraged, a growing confidence among the everyday Christian that he or she could readily understand the clear teaching of Scripture. Thus premillennial teaching and thought was a strong influence in the rise of Bible institutes throughout North America, as well as in the Bible conference movement. Premillennialism was strongly wed to a confidence in the verbally inspired, inerrant Word of God and gave impetus to the development of early twentieth-century fundamentalism.

This new movement also gave strength to a strong missions movement and evangelical thrust which ran counter to the progressive or postmillennial hopes for an advancing humanity. Premillennialism gave an answer to the false evolutionary hopes of Darwinism for the human race. "Far from paralyzing ... missionary effort," wrote Nathaniel West in 1879, "premillennial belief was . . . one of the mightiest incentives to earnestness in preaching the Gospel to every creature, until He comes, not to make the world better, but to save people out of the world."[30] Dr. A.B. Simpson saw a twofold incentive arising from what he called the blessed hope: encouraging a missionary message of warning, and also awakening and issuing a call to the practice of holiness in preparation for Christ's coming.[31] It was this renewed premillennialism, with its inclination for the clear, literal teaching of the Bible and a refocused mission to the world, that swept up new church movements in the late 1800s—including that movement which would become The Christian and Missionary Alliance.

4. Interpretations of Revelation 20:1-6

And I saw an angel coming down out of heaven, having the key to the Abyss and holding in his hand a great chain. He seized the dragon, that ancient serpent, who is the devil, or Satan, and bound him for a thousand years. He threw him into the Abyss, and locked and sealed it over him, to keep him from deceiving the nations anymore until the thousand years were ended. After that, he must be set free for a short time.

I saw thrones on which were seated those who had
been given authority to judge. And I saw the souls of
those who had been beheaded because of their testimony
for Jesus and because of the word of God. They had not
worshiped the beast or his image and had not received
his mark on their foreheads or their hands. They came to
life and reigned with Christ a thousand years. (The rest
of the dead did not come to life until the thousand years
were ended.) This is the first resurrection. The second
death has no power over them, but they will be priests of
God and of Christ and will reign with him for a thousand
years. (Revelation 20:1-6)

Dr. Simpson's and the Alliance belief in the millennium does
not rest on Revelation 20 alone, but on the numerous prophecies of the Old Testament that herald the coming Messiah who
will reign on David's throne and rule over a peaceful kingdom.
The truth of the Messianic age rests on the literal interpretation
of these many Old Testament passages. The primary contribution that Revelation 20:1-6 makes regarding the Messianic
Kingdom is to disclose its duration of 1,000 years. It should be
considered significant that this duration is mentioned six times
within this brief passage.

However, because the amillennial/postmillennial advocates
deny the relevance of Old Testament passages and promises
(conceiving all these promises either to be spiritually transferred to the Church where possible, or made null and void on
account of Israel's unbelief), the scriptural ground for the debate between them and premillennialists has been generally
narrowed down to Revelation 20:1-6. Therefore, a brief overview of the respective competing interpretations of this passage
is in order. This will be followed by a framing of the historic
expectation for a millennium that qualifies how the audience
was likely to read the author's intent.

Premillennial View

Chapter 19 is the key passage in Revelation describing the

second coming of Christ to earth. This second coming is a key theme of the book according to Revelation 1:7, "Look, he is coming. . . ." Chapter 20 follows in clear chronological order and describes two bodily resurrections separated by a period of 1,000 years. In between them, Satan shall be bound, and those first raised shall reign with Christ upon the earth. At the end of this time there shall be a brief release of Satan followed by his being cast into the Lake of Fire, the second resurrection and the final judgment. Then the eternal state shall be established.

Amillennial/Postmillennial View

As has already been observed, this interpretation of Revelation 20:1-6 finds its historical roots in the novel thinking of Augustine on the passage. The interpretation is figurative and not literal.

Chapter 20 is not viewed chronologically by the amillennialist nor by the postmillennialist as following chapter 19, but rather as a return to the time of the present period of the Church.

This would not be the natural rendering when considering the succession of *kai eidon* (And I saw) in Revelation 19:11, 17; 20:1, 4, 11; 21:1. This repeated phrase seems to introduce an unfolding series of interrelated visions which moves progressively forward, not retrogressively. With this understanding, the progressive sequence would then be obvious: the second coming, the judgment of the armies, the judgment of the Beast and the False Prophet in the lake of fire, the binding of Satan in the Abyss for 1,000 years, the reign of those participating in the first resurrection, the final judgment and the new heavens and new earth.

The 1,000 years are taken symbolically to mean the complete and full present state of the Church. Verses 1-3 would then refer to the present age here on earth with Satan bound from deceiving the nations and stopping the spread of the gospel. Verses 4-6 would refer to this same period in heaven with the departed souls of the redeemed with God.

The first resurrection is said to be a spiritual resurrection of souls into the presence of God. (Augustine added to this the spiritual resurrection of the redeemed on earth according to Ephesians 2:1). The second resurrection is the one general physical resurrection at the end of the age.

In response to this interpretation Henry Alford gave the well-known quote:

> If, in a passage where two resurrections are mentioned, where certain *psychai ezaesan* at the first, and the rest of the *nekoi ezesan* only at the end of a specified period after the first; if in such a passage the first resurrection may be understood to mean spiritual rising with Christ, while the second means literal rising from the grave, then there is an end of all significance in language, and Scripture is wiped out as a definite testimony to anything.[32]

Millennial Expectation and John's Intent in Revelation 20

There was a well established belief in the ancient world that there was to be a literal 1,000-year millennium of peace and righteousness upon the earth.

Bishop Russell of Scotland, an anti-millenarian, says:

> With respect to the millennium it must be acknowledged that the doctrine concerning it stretches back into antiquity so remote and obscure, that it is impossible to fix its origin. The tradition that the earth, as well as the moral and religious state of its inhabitants, were to undergo a great change at the end of 6,000 years, has been detected in the writing of Pagans, Jews and Christians. It is found in the most ancient of those commentaries of the Old Testament, which we owe to the learning of the Rabbinical school.[33]

Zoroaster, an ancient Persian philosopher, taught "in the end Sosioch [a name resembling in sound the Hebrew Messiah] makes his appearance, under whose reign the dead are raised, the judgment takes place, and the earth is renovated and glorified. . . . He also taught the six-millennial duration of the world."[34]

Theopompus, who flourished in 340 B.C., relates that the Persian Magi taught the present state of things would continue 6,000 years, after which Hades, or death, would be destroyed, and men would live happily. Bishop Russell, from whom we extract, adds that the opinion of the ancient Jews on this point may be gathered from the statement of a Rabbi who said, "The world endures 6000 years, and in the 1000, or millennium that follows, the enemies of God will be destroyed."[35]

The ancient Etruscans taught, "The world was formed in the course of six periods; each period comprehending a millenary; while 6000 years are allotted for a seventh period, viz, that of its duration."[36]

Rabbi Elias, a Jewish doctor of high antiquity, lived, says Bishop Russell, about 200 years before Christ. His opinion is called by the Jews, "A tradition of the house of Elias." He taught that the world would be "2000 years void of the law; 2000 years under the law, and 2000 years under the Messiah." He limited the duration of the world to 6,000 years and held that in the seventh millenary, "The earth would be renewed and the righteous dead raised; that these should not again be turned to dust, and that the just then alive should mount up with wings as the eagle: so that in that day they would not fear though the mountains be cast into the midst of the sea. Psalms 46:3."[37]

There was also a contemporary millennial expectation in John's day. Rabbi Gamaliel, the teacher of Paul, used the phrase "in the land that the LORD swore to give your forefathers" from Deuteronomy 11:21, to demonstrate the resurrection of the dead to silence the Sadducees. He said, "as Abraham, Isaac, and Jacob had it not; and God cannot lie; therefore, they must be raised from the dead to inherit it." The importance of this quotation proves that there was a real, literal—not figurative—anticipation of an earthly millennial reign in John's day.

Acts 1:6 is the last of many dialogues of expectation that the disciples had with Jesus on the subject. In each case Jesus never speaks to correct their core conviction of an expected physical kingdom but by implication or limited qualification seems to encourage it.

The Sibylline Oracles are frequently quoted by the early Church Fathers. They are a rare and ancient writing of Greek verse comprising fourteen books by various authors, some written before Christ and some after. These oracles, as well, taught of a coming millennium. This millennium with surrounding judgments is one of the strong themes of the oracles. (Paul quoted from these writings in Acts 17:28 and Titus 1:12).

Finally, it is well known that John's nemesis and Gnostic contemporary, Cerinthus (A.D., 100), taught of the coming of Jesus before 1,000 years of sensuous pleasure, after which there would be a consummation of this age.

In John's day there is little or no evidence that this period of 1,000 years of bliss was ever understood in any other way than the literal. The evidence abounds that such an interpretation and expectation was strongly set in the minds of his contemporaries. The weight of both the ancient expectation and the contemporary expectations makes it highly unlikely that John would have chosen to use such a culturally overloaded language unless he had intended not a figurative understanding, but a literal one. In the same way the audience that heard and read John would have been so primed by the contemporary expectation that they certainly would have received the millennial language in the framework of the popular literal expectation.

5. The Relevance of Premillennialism for the Future of The Christian and Missionary Alliance

A final consideration must be given to the value of this doctrine as it applies to The Christian and Missionary Alliance. Many of the views of Dr. A.B. Simpson on this topic and its relationship to the early Alliance were presented in response to the postmillennialism that was around at the end of the last century. This concept of postmillennialism was largely humanistic and promoted a social gospel ministry for the Church. Its confidence in the growth of the human spirit left one un-guarded against the darkness of his own nature, and unim-pressed with his need for the abundant life of Jesus within him which would enable him to please God. Here was an optimistic view of history that set, accidentally or not, man at its center. Dr. Simpson's view of history and what the future would even-tually comprise, however, required the active intervention and revelation of Jesus Christ.

Dr. Simpson was not so pessimistic that he saw the earth passing away without a golden age of historical peace and a reign of righteousness. He was not so optimistic that he saw that age coming by any other means than the intervention of the Son of God as King of the earth. In all this he looked be-yond to the great and final glory of the eternal state, where God, having brought in the ultimate expression of glory in history, would climax His display of glory throughout all eternity.

The Alliance teaching on the centrality of Christ in the his-tory of the world is evidenced by its unwillingness to be side-tracked into focusing upon God's dealing with the nation Israel as the primary key for understanding eschatology. Rather, the focus remained on Christ, the blessed Olive Root of the people of God and the basis of blessing for Jew and Gentile in every age and in the age to come. Together there would be one fold, regardless of the administration, in the millennium. This truth is expressed in the structure of the New Jerusalem where on the gates of the city are engraved the names of the twelve tribes of the sons of Israel and on the foundation stones are the names of the twelve apostles of the Lamb. In the city of God it is Jew and Gentile who will, when grafted into Christ, live as the people of God.[38]

Alliance Distinctives in Review

Now consider again the five distinctives introduced at the be-ginning of this paper in order to help answer the question, "How relevant is this doctrine in giving focus and direction to The Christian and Missionary Alliance?" Consider the follow-ing questions.

Is it possible to be motivated for missions and be either amillennial or postmillennial? Is it possible to issue a call for holiness through the abiding life of Christ and be either amillennial or postmillennial? Is it possible to develop a Christocentric view of history and be either amillennial or postmillennial? Is it possible to believe in the inerrant Word of God and be either amillennial or postmillennial? Is it possible to affirm the integrity of God and be either amillennial or postmillennial?

To all of these questions, in deference to both the amillennialist and the postmillennialist we must give a resounding "Yes."

The Transcendent Integrity of God

One should remember, however, that the early conviction of the Alliance was that the overriding purpose of human history was the glory of God, a public display of His integrity. This glory manifested in the Church, manifested in the Son and manifested in God's faithfulness to Israel was reflected in the premillennialism of the Alliance. Dr. Simpson wept when he read the Balfour Declaration to his congregation, following Allenby's taking of Jerusalem. That declaration stated, "His Majesty's Government views with favor the establishment in Palestine of a national home for the Jewish people. . . ." [39] Dr. Simpson later wrote, "Israel is going home and Christ is coming back again!" [40]

This same premillennial sentiment for God's glory and integrity is expressed by Marv Rosenthal when he writes,

> If God does not keep His word to Israel, He is not true. If God does not have power to fulfill His purposes, He is not omnipotent. If God does not know that certain things are going to occur and gets caught off guard, He is not omniscient. If God has wearied of Israel, He is not long-suffering. If God has changed His mind, He is not immutable. And in this we must be clear—if God has changed His mind in relation to His purpose for Israel, perhaps He will change His mind concerning His purposes for the Church. Perhaps we do not have a home in

glory land. Perhaps He is going to rescind His grace toward us. Enough! God is holy, just, true, loving, good, long-suffering, faithful, omnipotent, immutable, and infinitely more. In the first instance, the millennial issue is not prophetical, it is theological. It is not so much a consideration of what will happen tomorrow, it deals with what God's character is like today. Because He is a faithful God, He will keep His promises to Israel—that requires a literal, Millennial Kingdom established by the Lord Jesus Christ. God will keep His promises to the believer—that requires a home in glory in His presence forevermore.[41]

The Infallible Word of God

It must be recognized again that it was the belief of the founders of the Alliance that this teaching was true to the testimony of Scripture.[42] Among every other perceived advantage, it kept the Old Testament from becoming a deserted city, left only for Bible scholars and archaeologists to rummage through for relics of abandoned and voided hopes. Instead, the Old Testament remained a living testament to the sufficient and assured grace of Christ for every age and for the ages to come. As such, the whole of the Word of God is understood to be living and powerful and sharper than any two-edged sword and fit for every man and woman of God (see Hebrews 4:12).

Although Dr. Simpson was committed to the study of types within the Scripture, he held to the literal and historical nature of the Bible.[43] The great danger introduced by the combination of Darwinism, liberal theology, the Social Gospel and liberal biased critical Bible scholarship in Dr. Simpson's day was the erosion of long held beliefs. Along with this erosion, "Modernism" effectively removed the Word from the rank and file of Christianity and placed it in the hands of an elite "scholarship." Against this tide, premillennialism supported a countermovement of growing confidence in Scripture expressed in the belief that every part of the Bible could be understood in its literal and normal sense; that, excepting the cases of resulting absurdities, it should be taken literally. This confidence turned common people boldly back to the Word, and as they applied this principle of understanding the Scripture to both Old and New Testament prophecy, they saw written there the secrets of a coming millennial kingdom over which Christ would reign as King upon the earth.

Loraine Boettner, postmillennialist, recognizes this point of a literal, not letter-al, interpretation of prophecy when he admits that, "It is generally agreed that if the prophecies are taken literally, they do foretell a restoration of the nation of Israel in the land of Palestine with the Jews having a prominent place in that kingdom and ruling over the other nations."[44] This was a part of what the early Alliance saw in the millennium and what they invited its rank and file membership to see in their private and public study of the Bible.

The Centrality of Christ

The centrality of Christ was seen in His progressive goal for history climaxing in a reign of glory in which all the nations are subject to His rule of peace for 1,000 years. Today Christ's rule in history is the invisible reign within the hearts of God's children. This rule is hidden from the world's view. The rule of the eternal state shall be outside of history. But in history there shall be the final phase of time in which Christ shall rule from an earthly throne and display His glory over time, in time. Thus, nothing of the created order shall escape the full manifestation and reign of Christ's glory in it, not even time.

The millennium, ending in a final rebellion, will also serve to commend the justice of God on that last day of judgment. Man will have demonstrated, in that day, that his sin is due to nothing else than the depravity of his own heart. This fixed and progressive goal of history, that Christ shall be glorified and demonstrated as triumphant in time and place, was the hope of the early Church and the source of their encouragement in the face of a corrupt age. It was a hope renewed in the movement of the early Alliance.

The Christ-life

It was not the threat of judgment alone but the hopeful prospect of a historical holiness, a Christ-in-us-ness that should ultimately inspire God's children. Holiness in Jesus is not only a taste of finding heaven today, of living in the glory; it is the foreshadowing of a real and earthly reign of glory that we shall enjoy with Christ in time, on earth. Dr. Simpson wrote, "Because we are going to be like Him, then, we wear His image now. We anticipate our coming glory . . . so we try on even here the robes of our approaching coronation." [45]

Dr. Simpson pushed this application home strongly in his exposition of Isaiah 11: "We have no right to be looking for the millennium unless we have the millennium in our own hearts. We have no business to expect an eternity of peace if we are living in strife and envy now. Let us begin the millennial life here if we expect to enjoy it by and by." [46]

A Missionary Alliance

It is true that premillennialism teaches that the only hope for the future of the world is Christ, not Christianization. Therefore, people need to be saved out of the world. Yet there is as well the hopeful incentive that one day Christ will rule the nations and gather from them the fruit of worship from upon this earth, in time and as a goal of history. For the early Alliance each victory won overseas, and here, was a small foreshadowing of the triumph Jesus was bringing to earth and to eternity. Dr. Simpson's call to bring back the King was less the cry of desperation as it was a call to join in Christ's ultimate triumph.

It is possible to hold to these five passions for the integrity of God, the inerrancy of His Word, the centrality of His Son, the prospects of His sanctification and the supremacy of His mission apart from one's view of the millennium. Still, for the Alliance these passions have risen historically, not in spite of its eschatology, but in some ways uniquely because of it. These things are more closely related than we can appreciate at first or second glance. They are intertwined in a delicate cause and effect. We should devote ourselves to fully understand the role this position had in shaping our denominational distinctives and emphases. As the Alliance moves into a new century, in a check against historical drift, care must be taken not to cut the cords which bind us to the moorings of our movement even as we hold fast to that which is good.

> O Christ, my Lord and King, this is the prayer I bring,
> This is the song I sing: Thy Kingdom come.
> Help me to work and pray, help me to live each day,
> That all I do may say, Thy kingdom come.
> Upon my heart's high throne, rule Thou and Thou
>   alone;
> Let me be all Thine own! Thy kingdom come.
> Through all the earth abroad, wherever man has trod,
> Send forth Thy Word, O God, Thy kingdom come.
> Soon may our King appear! Haste bright millennial
>   year!
> We live to bring it near. Thy kingdom come.[47]

Endnotes

[1] Raymond Ludwigson, *A Survey of Bible Prophecy* (Grand Rapids, MI: Zondervan, 1978), 96.

[2] A.B. Simpson, *The Coming One* (New York: Christian Alliance Publishing, 1912), 7-18.

[3] Ibid., 16.

[4] Ibid., 152-153.

[5] George N.H. Peters, *The Theocratic Kingdom*, 3 vols. (Grand Rapids, MI: Kregel Publications, 1988), 449.

[6] D.T. Taylor, *The Voice of the Church on the Coming and Kingdom of the Redeemer or A History of the Doctrine of the Reign of Christ on the Earth* (Boston: H.L. Hastings, 1861), 52.

[7] Ludwigson, *A Survey of Bible Prophecy*, 127.

[8] Dr. Renald Showers, "A Description and Early History of Millennial Views," *Israel My Glory* (June 1986): 25.

[9] David Larsen, *Jews, Gentiles and the Church* (Grand Rapids: Discovery House Publishing, 1995), 120, citing Tertullian, *Against Marcion* 7.5.9.

10 Brian E. Daley, *The Hope of the Early Church: A Handbook of Patristic Eschatology* (Cambridge: Cambridge University Press, 1992), 61.

11 Ibid.

12 Ibid., 68.

13 Paul Boyer, *When Time Shall Be No More* (Cambridge, MA: The Belknap Press of Harvard University Press, 1992), 49.

14 E.A. Pinell, *Christian League Newsletter on The Millennial vs. Amillennial Debate*, 1980, 9.

15 Ibid.

16 Larsen, *Jews, Gentiles and the Church*, 122.

17 Augustine, *The City of God*, in *The Nicene and Post-Nicene Fathers*, Philip Schaff, ed. (Grand Rapids, MI: Eerdmans, 1979), series I, vol. II. ed., 426.

18 E.A. Pinell, *Christian League Newsletter*, 10.

19 Walter Elwell, *The Concise Evangelical Dictionary of Theology*, 314.

20 A revealing study of Augustine's Neoplatonism is found in Robert J. O'Connell, *St. Augustine's Early Theory of Man.*

21 Anthony Hoekema, *The Bible and the Future* (Grand Rapids: Eerdmans, 1979), 183.

22 Boyer, *When Time Shall Be No More*, 50.

23 Elwell, *The Concise Evangelical Dictionary of Theology*, 314.

24 Larsen, *Jews, Gentiles and the Church*, 123.

25 Taylor, *The Voice of the Church on the Coming and Kingdom of the Redeemer*, 200-201.

26 Larsen, *Jews, Gentiles and the Church*, 124.

27 Ibid., 127.

28 Ibid., 126.

29 Boyer, *When Time Shall Be No More*, 89.

30 Ibid., 97, quoting *Premillennial Essays* by West.

31 Simpson, *The Coming One*, 201.

32 Robert G. Clouse, *The Meaning of the Millennium: Four Views* (Downers Grove, IL: InterVarsity, 1977), 37-38. The quote of Henry Alford is cited by George Eldon Ladd.

33 D.T. Taylor, *The Voice of the Church on the Coming and Kingdom of the Redeemer*, 25, citing Bishop Russell from *Discourse on the Millennium*, 39.

34 Ibid., 28, citing Dr. Hengstenberg in *Christology*, vol. 1, 16. Dr. Hengstenberg thinks Zoroaster stole and adulterated the truths of Revelation.

[35] Ibid., 27.

[36] Ibid., 28.

[37] Ibid., 25-26.

[38] Keith Bailey, *Christ's Coming and His Kingdom* (Camp Hill, PA: Christian Publications, 1981). Chapter six, entitled "The Rich Root of the Olive Tree," is a wonderfully sweet discussion on this matter and resounds with a feel of the central glory of Alliance Christology applied to eschatology.

[39] Abba Eban, *Heritage: Civilization and the Jews* (New York: Summit Books, 1984), 256.

[40] Simpson, *The Coming One*, 192.

[41] Marv Rosenthal, "The Importance of a Premillennial Theology," *Israel My Glory* (October 1986): 7.

[42] The hermeneutical assessment of the basis of premillennialism is bound up in an understanding that the 1,000 years referenced in Revelation 20:1-7 is a literal period of 1,000 years. For a thorough presentation of the literal interpretation of these passages see Robert L. Thomas, *Revelation, An Exegetical Commentary* (Moody Press, 1995), vol. 2, 403-423 and also Excursus 4 at the end of volume 2. The author states

> Chronological sequence is the natural understanding of the visions. Also the Old Testament framework that supplies the foundation for this book requires a future period on earth to fulfill the promises of a Messianic age. It is a structural necessity of Revelation that this 1000 years lies in the future too. . . . If the writer (John) wanted a symbolic number why did he not use 144,000 (cf. 7:1; 14:1), 200,000,000 (9:16), "ten thousand times ten thousand, and thousands of thousands" (5:11) or an incalculably large number (7:9)? The fact is that no number in Revelation is verifiably a symbolic number. On the other hand, nonsymbolic usage of numbers is the rule."

For a concise summary of the genre and hermeneutic of Revelation and further study for the compelling case of a literal interpretation see *Revelation, An Exegetical Commentary*, vol. 1, 23-39.

[43] A.B. Simpson, *Divine Emblems* (Camp Hill, PA: Christian Publications, 1995), 9.

[44] Clouse, *The Meaning of the Millennium: Four Views*, 95.

[45] Simpson, *The Coming One*, 203.

[46] A.B. Simpson, *Christ in the Bible Series—Isaiah* (Harrisburg, PA: Christian Publications, n.d.), 146.

[47] A.B. Simpson, *Songs of the Spirit* (Harrisburg, PA: Christian Publications, 1920), 122.

Approximating the Millennium: Premillennial Evangelicalism and Racial Reconciliation

Douglas Matthews

1. The Premillennial Addiction to Darkness and the Issue of Racial Reconciliation

Twentieth-century racism has been omnipresent—unlike the kingdom of God. Bosnia-Herzegovina. Hitler. Palestine. Lebanon. Israel. O.J. Simpson. Los Angeles. Ruby Ridge.[1] Louis Farrakhan. Africa. George Wallace. Birmingham. Rodney King. Little Rock, Arkansas. Auschwitz.

Is there a distinctively Christian message for a century erupting with ethnic conflict? Does the premillennial Christian Church have a relevant message? Indeed it does, if the premillennial Church can exorcise its speculative, fatalistic, otherworldly and escapist demons[2] and learn to take seriously its own doctrine of the future millennium. In the millennial *telos* (consummation), the line of promise of Abraham's true, multi-racial, obedient seed engages in a celebration of the Lamb's victory and participates in a lengthy historical and earthly existence. Ladd, Cullman and Beasley-Murray[3] have provided a theological foundation for affirming that premillennialism's utopia is a future global and concretized manifestation of the rule of God. Indeed, this already-but-not-yet kingdom rule—a rule which excludes racism—has enveloped the present aeon. The millennial rule can be viewed in socio-eschatological terms

71

as a moral imperative and spiritual reality which is approximately evident in the present age—even beyond the walls of the Church.

Walter Rauschenbusch, who did not embrace premillennialism, sensed the import of the doctrine of the millennium and called for "a restoration of the millennial hope" which "was crude in its form but wholly right in its substance."[4] Such a hope, he argued, safeguarded the dignity of "every least human being" and contributed to the realization of the brotherhood of man.[5] The doctrine of the millennium is actually an explosive and prophetic concept. The utopian *telos* provides hope, engenders *eschatopraxis*,[6] and also warns, like Damocles' sword hanging by a single hair, of the coming judgment on evils such as racism. A commitment to a properly conceptualized earthly utopia negates otherworldliness and fosters concern for God's creation, including cultural and social life.[7] The transformed world *is* our home. Hence, premillennialists may be able to affirm sincerely that racial reconciliation is the future, and the future is now.

This statement about racial reconciliation, which can be appropriated by a modified premillennialism, reflects the type of eschatological story that partially contributed to liberating the captives in previous generations. Thus, Jurgen Moltmann rightly argues that "Christianity is eschatology through and through—namely, a world transforming and world overcoming hope."[8]

Martin Luther King, Jr., illustrated Moltmann's point with his somewhat idealistic and utopian hope for the future—and yet the real world at least partially changed. King sounds the eschatological note:

> I have a dream that one day on the red hills of Georgia the sons of former slaves and sons of former slave owners will be able to sit down together at the table of brotherhood.
>
> I have a dream that one day even the state of Mississippi, a desert state sweltering with the heat of injustice

and oppression, will be transformed into an oasis of freedom and justice. . . .

I have a dream today.

I have a dream that one day every valley shall be ex-
alted, every hill made low, the rough places will be made
plains, and the crooked places will be made straight, and
the glory of the Lord shall be revealed, and all flesh shall
see it together.

This is our hope. This is the faith with which I return
to the South. With this faith we will be able to hew out of
the mountain of despair a stone of hope. With this faith
we will be able to transform the jangling discords of our
nation into a beautiful symphony of brotherhood. With
this faith we will be able to work together, to pray together, to struggle together, to go to jail together, to
stand up for freedom together, knowing that we will be
free one day.[9]

Is this dream an empty, dangerously naive hope or a liberating
vision?

In *Uncle Tom's Cabin,* first published in the 1850s, Harriet
Beecher Stowe well illustrates the type of captivating and
praxis-provoking vision of hope and judgment which mobilized
masses of evangelicals[10] to seek social justice and abolish slavery. Stowe writes:

This is an age of the world when nations are trembling
and convulsed. A mighty influence is abroad, surging
and heaving the world, as with an earthquake. And is
America safe? Every nation that carries in its bosom
great and unredressed injustice has in it the elements of
this last convulsion.

For what is this mighty influence thus rousing in all
nations and languages those groanings that cannot be ut-
tered, for man's freedom and equality?

O, Church of Christ, read the signs of the times! Is not
this power the spirit of HIM whose kingdom is yet to

come, and whose will to be done on earth as it is in heaven?

But who may abide the day of his appearing? "For that day shall burn as an oven: and he shall appear as a swift witness against those that oppress the hireling in his wages, the widow and the fatherless, and that *turn aside the stranger in his right:* and he shall break in pieces the oppressor."

Are not these dread words for a nation bearing in her bosom so mighty an injustice? Christians! every time that you pray that the kingdom of Christ may come, can you forget that prophecy associates, in dread fellowship, the *day of vengeance* with the year of his redeemed?

A day of grace is yet held out to us. Both North and South have been guilty before God; and the *Christian Church* has a heavy account to answer. Not by combining together, to protect injustice and cruelty, and making a common capital of sin, is this Union to be saved,—but by repentance, justice, and mercy; for, not surer is the eternal law by which the millstone sinks in the ocean, than the stronger law, by which injustice and cruelty shall bring on nations the wrath of Almighty God![11]

Stowe uses the fear of eschatological judgment, the "signs of the times," not to promote escapism but instead to encourage orthodoxy and orthopraxy.

Donald Dayton, in *Discovering Our Evangelical Heritage,* and Timothy Smith, in *Revivalism and Social Reform,*[12] have documented how the powerful eschatological impulse was harnessed in the churches behind a vision that energized social reform movements. The faithful passionately and sacrificially exemplified the theology of the cross while pursuing a better world now. Is this the purpose that eschatology serves in the evangelical Church today?

Both King and Stowe attempted to apply central biblical and Christian eschatological conceptions to the Church and American society. Consider the following biblical motifs relative to the racial question. The author of Revelation looks forward to a day on this planet when all races will celebrate the victory of the Lamb:

> You are worthy to take the scroll
> and to open its seals,
> because you were slain,
> and with your blood you purchased men for God
> from every tribe and language and people and nation.
> You have made them to be a kingdom and priests
> to serve our God,
> and they will *reign on the earth*.
> (5:9-10, emphasis added)

Paul argues that racism has been abolished in the eschatological, already-but-not-yet, Christ event: "There is neither Jew nor Greek, slave nor free, male nor female, for you are all one in Christ Jesus" (Galatians 3:28). This eschatological passage teaches that Abraham's true seed is based upon a spiritual relationship and therefore is multiracial. Peter's vision in Acts 10 illustrates the truth that the eschatological King and Judge accepts all who believe and receive "forgiveness of sins through his name," regardless of race or color (10:42-43).

Racism may continue in the present age, but, theologically, it is passing away. The Savior taught that the meek and those who love their neighbors, even if they are of a different race, are Abraham's true seed and will inherit the earth. The biblical witness affirms that those who despise meekness, refuse to forgive others, hate their neighbor or their brother (1 John) and practice "hatred" (Galatians 5:20) will not inherit the kingdom of God. These unbelievers lack true, biblical and saving faith. Stated succinctly, racists, Nazis, neo-Nazis, the Klan and those engaging in ethnic cleansing will not inherit the kingdom of God now or ever.[13] The coming global concretized manifestation of the kingdom, a kingdom which already has decisively intruded into the here and now, excludes racism.

The eschatologically pre-utopian branch of evangelicalism[14] may find such noble and transformational programs to be simple-minded and hopelessly idealistic. Within premillennial evangeli-calism the powerful and history-changing eschatological impulse is often either dead or directed toward superficial last-days evan-gelism and sensationalistic Lindseyism. In radical contrast to Jurgen Moltmann's eschatology, which calls the Church to see and participate with God in human suffering and liberation, Dar-byism (dispensationalism) views historic tragedies as evidence of Satan's present rule and the imminent escape of the Church from the world. Moltmann's Divine Pathos for the oppressed is often replaced with premillennial apathy for the dying world and an exuberance for escapism and soul-snatching. Of course their world, the world of conservative Protestant cultural dominance, is dying. Both Darbyism and Moltmann's Theology of Hope re-flect questionable theological extremes, with the latter emphasiz-ing the Divine Pathos to the point of affirming a pantheistic conception of suffering and evil. This contrast between Darbyism and Hope, however, suggests that an eschatological shift within premillennialism might also birth a new premillennial concep-tion of God as one who is involved and responsive. Shirley Guthrie, in the April 1996 issue of *Theology Today*, describes how a speculative doctrine of the sovereignty of God distances God from weakness, pain, evil, suffering and death.[15] If premillennial-ists begin to see God as truly at work, already, in the deepest pits of human sin and suffering, then their orthodox theism may take on a less speculative and more biblical hue.[16]

At the present time, however, many premillennialists might raise a series of troubling questions for those calling for racial reconciliation. They might agree with Harold Hoehner's cri-tique of evangelical efforts at making major social changes: "I think the whole thing is wrong-headed," he contends. "I just can't buy their basic presupposition that we can do anything significant to change the world. And you can waste an awful lot of time trying."[17] Why should one be deeply committed to a lengthy and arduous social program if one is certain of being raptured from earth before the end of the decade? Would not a serious interaction with culture be an act of spiritual unfaithfulness if, in these "last days," Satan's grip on civilization is nearly total? Perhaps such anti-utopians might see some value in pursuing racial healing within the Church. However, given the complexities and deep-rooted social realities that contribute to racism, it likely would be considered as somewhat utopian and a waste of evangelistic energies to seek widespread reconciliation, even in the increasingly apostate Church, in this present evil age.

Consider the types of queries relative to social concern that are consistent with the very titles of best-selling evangelical books. Walk with me into your local Christian bookstore. These premillennial evangelicals might ask the following: Are not the writings of educated Christian scholars who call for social change very possibly the writings of heretical liberals during *This Present Darkness?* Is not our idiot, postmodern, racist culture merely a divinely determined prophetic fulfillment that is keeping schedule with *The Divine Clock?* Are not the worldwide troubles and the urban decadence of this generation an assurance that the faithful will soon *Escape the Coming Night?* And since this is *The Late Great Planet Earth,* and we already have passed through *The Terminal Generation*[18] as the historical sunset draws nigh at *The End of the Age,* should not the Church abandon serious social, cultural and intellectual efforts in favor of more urgent tasks? Are not social reformists like Martin Luther King, Jr., calling for Christians to engage in civilization building coterminous with civilization's divinely planned collapse just prior to *The Final Battle?* Why not agree with the man who greatly shaped the premillennial psyche and modern revivalism, D.L. Moody, when he defined his social agenda, eschato-ecclesiology and eschato-evangelism by stating the following: "I look on this world as a wrecked vessel. God has given me a life-boat, and said to me, 'Moody, save all you can.' "[19] Is it any wonder that Moody eschewed intellectual culture, large-scale social concern and even theology?[20] If one follows Moody, should not evangelical energies be employed in the pragmatic task of eschatological apologetics,[21] evangelism and missions?

Shouldn't Christians boldly proclaim a *Final Warning* so that those who believe will not be *Left Behind*? Is it appropriate to expend useless time and resources on the complexities of political philosophy, race relations or the fine points of cultural aesthetics given the *Signs of the Times*? Tim Lahaye's recent book, *No Fear of the Storm: Why Christians Will Escape All the Tribulation,* may or may not be a psychological panacea for those who want to abandon social reform, but it certainly is not a recipe for pre-Parousia social activism. Perhaps the book title *Heaven: Your Real Home* best captures the eschatological and otherworldly spirit of hordes of evangelicals as we approach the next millennium.[22] It is not unlikely that an unfortunate event of chemical or nuclear terrorism will take place within the next few decades. If this happens, especially if this happens in the Middle East, eschatomania will probably be energized as never before, unless the Church educates and prepares for these types of events now.

Reflection upon the amentality of the pre-utopian Church may cause the term pathology to come to mind. Millard Erickson uses the term "eschatomania"[23] as a descriptor of the outlook of many of these evangelicals. Whatever term is used to describe such a vision of the future, it is difficult to see how racial reconciliation could become a priority for Lindseyan evangelicals. An eschatological revolution may have to precede mental renewal, ecclesial renewal and social engagement.

2. The Scandal of Fat Premillennial Minds, Tepid Hearts and Atrophied Hands

The pathology of some variants of premillennial evangelicalism reinforces other evangelical weaknesses that obstruct coherent social concern. In recently published books, Mark Noll and Os Guiness have specified areas of weakness which hinder an evangelical intellectual renaissance. These encumbrances also inhibit the development and acceptance of a sophisticated and comprehensive theology of racial reconciliation. Noll and Guiness rightly complain about evangelical anti-intellectualism, immediatism, hyper-individualism, naive common sense philosophy, a polarized view of truth, anti-cultural separatism, anti-theological pietism, simplistic primitivism, anti-urban populism, excessively pragmatic evangelism and a resulting crude philistinism.[24] We're in bad shape. Many of these characteristics directly undermine a concern for racial reconciliation and the plight of broken and oppressed peoples. Not only have many of these hindrances become institutionalized in some premillennial variations, but they are often reinforced and sometimes logical concomitants of prevailing evangelical eschatologies. Isaac Rottenberg comments:

> When the "not yet" is stressed at the expense of the "already," the world tends to be viewed as being under the rule of Satan, and a spirit of escapism and other-worldliness often prevails. There is much talk about heaven and the hopelessness of any human efforts to establish a more just social order.[25]

A reconstructed premillennialism may be required for a renewed evangelical mind, and a renewed mind is a critical prerequisite and stable resource for a long-term program of racial reconciliation in the Church and society.

Eschatomania, as Vernon Grounds has rightly observed, sometimes unwittingly lends "substance to the communist indictment of religion as an opiate, a drug which induces hallucinatory dreams, causing its addicts to forget the harsh circumstances around them."[26] This opiate undermines mental renewal, justifies status-quoism and produces a tepid faith that lacks zeal and does not work to alleviate the larger social problems of the needy and the abused. Head, heart and hand often remain underdeveloped due to this frenzied eschatology which also can serve as an oppressive story.[27]

The scandal of the evangelical mind is, in many respects, the scandal of the premillennial mind.[28] The recently proposed overhauls or fine-tunings of evangelicalism, such as Noll's *The Scandal of the Evanglical Mind*, may be inhibited apart from widespread eschatological revisioning. Is it possible that the critical vitality of an evangelical metamorphosis is the necessary resource of pre-utopian kingdom eschatology? The evangelical commitment to racial reconciliation requires a praxis-provoking, eschatologically oriented renewal that warms the heart and engages the head and hand.

3. The Hegemony of the Premillennial Story

The pre-utopian or premillennial story of the future probably reigns supreme in American evangelicalism and has enraptured the imagination of millions worldwide. Timothy Weber, altering and paraphrasing an old and "unsanitary" observation of H.L. Mencken, quips that "it would be hard to spit into a crowd of evangelicals these days without hitting a premillennialist." Weber continues:

> They seem to be everywhere. They get more headlines, buy more television time, and sell more books than anyone else around. Nearly all the celebrities of the electronic church preach premillennialism. . . .[29]

Hal Lindsey's speculative premillennial work *The Late Great Planet Earth* was reported to be the number one nonfiction bestseller, next to the Bible, in the decade prior to Reagan's presidency, with total sales at present approaching 30 million copies.[30] President Ronald Reagan frequently articulated premillennial and apocalyptic themes, and appointed premillennialists to high positions.[31] Premillennial evangelist Billy Graham stayed, prayed and consulted with President George Bush the night prior to the bombing of Baghdad that precipitated direct American involvement in the Gulf War. Weber has documented that all major evangelists and those most active in evangelism and missions since the late nineteenth century have subscribed to the premillennial story. He concludes: "Premillennialism's popular support is enormous."[32] Surveys of Fuller Seminary alumni and the constituency of *Christianity Today* reveal that a substantial majority embrace premillennialism, and many view eschatology as important to the way in which they live out their Christian lives.[33] Paul Boyer's recent Harvard

University Press publication, *When Time Shall Be No More*,[34] persuasively demonstrates how scholars have underestimated the pervasiveness and influence of apocalyptic premillennialism in American culture. Premillennialists may take power as never before if recent conservative victories in the House and Senate can be augmented by success in the upcoming presidential and state elections. Eschatology may have an uninterrupted connection to congressional and executive politics and policies that profoundly impact urban centers, minorities and the poor.

4. The Impact of Future-Stories on Real People

The widespread popularity of premillennial or anti-utopian eschatology[35] touches and often directs the lives of real people. Marcy's life is illustrative. She argued that spending years at college studying history, the arts and sciences made no sense. Why become an intellectual master of culture if culture is self-destructing? It is the Lord's job to fix everything (notice the passive posture) when He returns. It was 1987 when Marcy was contemplating attending college. Marcy's church had been preaching and teaching a new book, entitled *88 Reasons Why the Rapture Will Be in '88.*[36] To enroll in college for four years of study was futile since she would be raptured within a year or so. In spite of the fact that she was a brilliant, near-genius high school student she chose not to attend college—or to bother herself with civilization-saving or building.

Dr. Johnson also was quite brilliant and evidenced a commanding grasp of the flow of history and ideas. His response, however, to contemporary developments such as resurgent racism or the emergence of the supposed postmodern era of philosophy and culture was not an attempt to impact the thinking of the Academy. Instead, he repeatedly announced that these recent trends were strong evidence that the last generation had arrived. Postmodernity was viewed as the intellectual foundation of the collapse of civilization and the catalyst for Antichrist's rise to power and the Great Tribulation. Resurgent racism was considered as a possible prelude to an end-times helter-skelter. Even though Dr. Johnson was not a full-fledged traditional dispensationalist, he had absorbed enough elements of the ideology to preach gloom and doom. Like many non-dispensational evangelicals, he was still in a wide orbit around old Dallas Theological Seminary, the star of dispensationalists.

David and Steve also loved soul-saving. They were in Bible college, but they were very, very frustrated. As the bombs began to fall on Baghdad during the Gulf War, and as the Israelis donned gas masks live on CNN, they could not help but feel that they were wasting their time learning history, philosophy, literature and, yes, even theology. David lamented, "Why can't I just take the required courses in Bible, pastoral ministry and evangelism so I can go directly into serving Jesus after a year or two? The world is about to end and I'm diagramming sentences and reading Sartre." A friend, John, counseled David by suggesting that "the Lord has put you on the shelf for a while in college so you can mature spiritually."[37] Social issues such as racism were not even on the back burner of their minds.

These life stories of anti-utopian evangelicals stand in stark contrast to those of utopian evangelicals. Consider countless nineteenth- and twentieth-century believers, like Martin, Elijah P. Lovejoy or the Tappan brothers, who sometimes shed their blood or sacrificially contributed their lives and resources while attempting to bring God's rule to America in their century. It is a tragedy and, ironically, a utopian fallacy to devalue their contributions because they may have been overly utopian. They changed the world. They saw the world from the vantage point of what it could be, should be and will be, and took up their cross to realize the future in the present. For them, the kingdom was a present possibility, for Christ's triumph was very real and had multiple this-worldly implications, including racial reconciliation.

These stories reflect the experiences of real people who have been impacted by the very influential ideas of some variety of eschatology. Ideas are immensely powerful, especially visions of the future. Emerson says, "Beware when the Great God lets loose a thinker on this planet. Then all things are at risk. The very hopes of man, the thoughts of his heart, the religion of nations, the manners and morals of mankind are all at the mercy of a new generalization." Napoleon observes that "There are two powers in the world, the sword and the mind. In the long run, the sword is always beaten by the mind." Moore and Bruder summarize the thesis of the power of ideas: "For a revolution you need more than economic problems and guns. You need a philosophy. Wars are founded on a philosophy, or on efforts to destroy one. Communism, capitalism, fascism, humanism, Marxism—philosophies all of them. *Philosophies give birth to civilizations. They also end them*"[38] (italics mine). It should be noted that Moore and Brooder's list of secular philosophies is also a list of secular eschatologies that have captured the mind, allegiance and heroic obedience of millions. Future-stories are central to the programs and behavioral patterns of individuals, groups and nations. Personal, familial, communal, national and global eschatologies rule—consider Waco, Ruby Ridge or the New World Order. A new pre-utopian story could create a theological environment conducive to a culturally and intellectually dynamic evangelicalism. Unfortunately, evangelicals in this generation have been lured into inaction or incoherence by some aspects of the very sensationalistic *Late Great Planet Earth* amentality. This amentality is a critical factor in creating evangelical apathy toward race relations and it also contributes to the scandal of an evangelical mind often incapable of seriously grappling with critical social issues.

5. The Eschatological Options for Scandalizing the Scandal

Perhaps, some might argue, premillennialism should be abandoned. Our passions, thoughts, actions and understanding of the Church will follow our eschatological *telos*. Maybe the best way to scandalize the scandal is to consider adopting other views of Christ's return and rule.

Post-Utopianism and Neo-Post-Utopianism

Premillennialism could be discarded in favor of a post-utopian view of Christ's earthly rule (postmillennialism or neo-postmillennialism), but a strong biblical (see Ladd or

83

Beasley-Murray), historical and philosophical case can be made for retaining the general pre-utopian framework. Such a lengthy argument transcends the scope of this paper. However, premillennialism's best defense may not be the detailed exegesis of Revelation 20. Indeed, millennialism's best apologia is its consistency with these biblical mega-themes: 1) the recalcitrancy of the human heart; 2) the certainty of a post-Parousia transformed and ameliorated earthly existence that fulfills biblical hope and undergirds the value and meaning of earthly, historical, cultural and political realities; and 3) the certainty that only another event of the magnitude of the incarnation can establish paradise on earth. Scripture affirms that Paradise lost becomes paradise regained, and D-day advances to V-day *in* history and *on* earth.[39] Even the urban is transformed as the heavenly city comes to earth. Rather than reviving postmillennialisms or utopianisms that conflict with the biblical and historical data, it seems best to absorb the spirit and zeal of activist utopianism within a modified pre-utopian model.[40]

Post-utopianism should be credited with motivating the masses and taking the creation, incarnation and consummation seriously. These utopians often have been zealously *optimistic* and *worldly* (in the biblical sense of loving the creation). *Naive Post-Utopianism* was prevalent in the nineteenth and early twentieth century, but was eventually crushed by the realities of the Civil War, massive immigration, industrialization, urbanization and twentieth-century brutalities. Naive Post-Utopianism imbibed deeply of the triumphalistic spirit of modernity. *Shrewd Post-Utopianism* (or neo-post-utopianism or neo-post-millennialism) is primarily a post-Auschwitz phenomenon. These utopians try to transcend a static realism and remain optimistic while also avoiding a naive anthropology. They usually de-emphasize or deny an actual, historical Parousia. Utopia is preceded by many setbacks, difficult to attain, requires great self-denial and may be historically distant. Teilhard de Chardin even considers the possibility of a nuclear annihilation of the noosphere (the evolved mental realm) and the biosphere (the evolved biological realm), even though the divine lure would return to Eden once again in the event of such a calamity. Jurgen Moltmann's thought would exemplify many aspects of the shrewd post-utopian story.

What are some of the major liabilities of most expressions of utopianism today? 1) *The Utopian Fallacy.* Utopians negatively judge Dr. King's reforms, nineteenth-century reforms, America and its political and economic system, and clumsy first attempts at racial reconciliation (Promise Keepers) by comparing these realities to lofty and largely unattainable standards of perfection. Marxism and many modernistic utopianisms have used this illogic to enslave millions. 2) *The Anthropological Fallacy.* Utopians properly and prophetically critique the sinfulness and shortcomings of the ideology or praxis of others but fail to apply the same standards to themselves or their own crusades and stories. Messiah complexes often result. Sometimes we need to deconstruct the power game or ego trip cleverly hidden in our zealous deconstruction of others. Our deconstruction may be just another oppressive alternative narrative. 3) *The Programmatic Fallacy.* Utopians may inappropriately pursue worthy programs and goals. Perhaps the War on Poverty of the 1960s or the push for rapid and total integration fall into this category.

It will be argued below that a correct understanding of history inherent within a reconstructed pre-utopianism maintains the prophetic zeal and idealism of utopianism while cautiously avoiding the many liabilities of utopianism.

Non-Utopianism

A second major eschatological option is the non-utopian view of Christ's earthly rule. In other words, there is no earthly rule of Christ; there is no millennium. Non-utopianism or amillennialism is a commendable and balanced system that often avoids the excesses of rival eschatologies. It should be noted that it can also degenerate into speculation and pessimism as well, which is evidenced by amillennial prognostications from the early Protestant reformers to the present, including Harold Camping's 1994 pronouncements.[41] Unfortunately, the traditional non-utopian teaching concerning the post-Parousia era, which lacks an earthly reign of Christ, seems overly discontinuous with previous historical existence, catastrophic, otherworldly and fails to provide an adequate *telos* for present intellectual and cultural endeavors. Unlike pre-utopianism, non-utopianism denies the existence of an intermediate era (the millennium) which raises earthly and historical existence to the next level. Two currents of thought seem to exist within non-utopianism. The first is *Otherworldly Non-Utopianism*, where one's hope and concern is focused almost exclusively on another supersensory realm. Some representatives of the medieval monastic tradition gravitated in this direction. The second approach is an *Earthy Non-Utopianism*, where the importance and relationship between the two realms (heavenly and earthly) are maintained in tension or paradox. Reinhold Niebuhr's political realism is illustrative of many aspects of earthy non-utopianism. Martin Luther partially illustrates the earthy approach by suggesting that if he knew that the Lord's return would take place tomorrow, he would plant a tree today.[42] In contrast to Luther, many pre-utopians would frantically evangelize and distribute rapture tickets if they knew that only hours remained before phase one of the Lord's return (the rapture).

Pre-Utopianism

The last major socio-eschatological option is pre-utopianism. This semantic shift from premillennialism to pre-utopianism is intentional and important. The term premillennialism has become so associated with Lindseyan speculation that it has lost its socio-eschatological relevance. Pre-utopianism, however, interjects the social goal of utopia into the heart of eschatological thinking. We live on the verge, or on the edge (theologically and metaphysically), of utopia or fulfilled earthly existence. The world is being transformed and in due time will reach its appointed goal.

Those who give no serious consideration to this pre-utopian option frequently fail to recognize that there are many varieties of premillennial theology and social concern,[43] some of which do not require pessimism, escapism or anti-intellectualism. Os Guiness observes: "Premillennialism, I stress once more, is not itself the problem."[44] For example, the premillennialism of G.E. Ladd, Millard Erickson and Carl F.H. Henry avoids such speculation and pessimism. Erickson, as noted above, refers to such speculation as "eschatomania," and defends a post-tribulational rapture.[45] This view of the rapture implies that believers have a great deal at stake in preventing the putrefaction of Western culture and civilization. Another positive development in evangelicalism is Progressive Dispensationalism. This movement is traveling beyond many of the errors of the past and could embrace a coherent and comprehensive social ethic which will move away from otherworldliness, fatalism, speculation, literalism, the relegating of biblical and social imperatives to a past or future age and escapism.

Debates concerning whether premillennialism entails social inertia are intellectually inchoate and generally confused. First, a distinction must be made between the tendencies of a theology and the practices of an adherent. For example, a premillennialist may, incoherently, both affirm with confidence that Christ will return before 2000 and engage in long-term social programming. Sometimes a theology does undermine long-term social concern, but other personal or ideological factors have counteracted or muted the theology. Second, the claim that premillennial theology or practice either does or does not entail social inertia is meaningless unless one defines exactly what is meant by concepts such as social inertia or social concern. For example, a premillennialist may be very consistent with his or her pessimistic theology and serve in a soup kitchen or mission to the poor that attempts to snatch souls from the sinking ship called planet earth. Premillennialists have engaged in very courageous relief-oriented social concern over the last 100 years.[46] Therefore, it is imperative that critics of premillennialism delineate and distinguish among the theological tendencies and varieties, the practices and the multiple types of premillennial social concern.

These variations relative to social concern usually have been

ignored by scholars. Martin Marty's description of premillennialism as "a pessimistic view of human history"[47] illustrates this
tendency in academia to treat premillennialism as a monolithic
entity. Premillennialists have earned such disdain, however, in
view of statements such as the following by John Walvoord:
"Things are going to get worse and worse. There will be more
oppression, more injustice, more immorality as the age wears
on."[48] Consider the message that this statement sends to the
churches in the age of O.J.

Time and space limitations prohibit a full discussion, but
over the last 100 years premillennialists have adopted a variety
of social postures or strategies: 1) Antagonistic; 2) Symptomatic
or Relief-Oriented; 3) Preservative (with coherent and incoherent subvarieties); 4) Transformational or Conversionist (with
strategic subvarieties such as: evangelistic, discipleship, ecclesial, structural or incoherent postures); and 5) Influential-
Transformational (the view of this author).[49]

Pre-utopianism may be salvageable and even superior to
post-utopianism and non-utopianism. The debate about
which story of the future is preferred will not be resolved in
the present age. In sum, however, premillennial eschatology is
pre-utopian. Humanity exists in the era prior to utopia on
earth. The biblical literature, the theology of the ante-Nicene
Church and empirical historical realities all herald the truth
that an event of the theological magnitude of the incarnation
must precede the restoration of paradise on earth. Postmillennialism is post-utopian theology, and while avoiding otherworldliness it fails to recognize that only an event like the
Parousia can spark the totality of the millennium on this
planet. The amillennial future-vision, somewhat Greek or Platonic in its denial of an earthly reign of Christ, is non-utopian, for there is no actual, historical millennium. The
non-utopian, while usually avoiding excessive pessimism and
naive optimism (the wheat and tares will grow together until
the harvest), unknowingly devalues the creation, the mean-
ingfulness of history and the biblical hope of a paradise regained in this world. Earthy non-utopians are exempt from

the full force of these criticisms, but their system still retains excessive otherworldliness by affirming such a catastrophic conception of the Parousia. History is catapulted from the present age into the eternal state in one quantum leap. Alva J. McClain has argued that this view empties history of meaning. Human history is a stairway leading nowhere: "History becomes the preparatory 'vestibule' of eternity, and not a very rational vestibule at that. It is a narrow corridor, cramped, and dark, a kind of 'waiting room,' leading nowhere *within* the historical process, but only fit to be abandoned at last for an ideal existence on another plane."[50]

A strong exegetical case can and has been made for pre-utopianism by G.E. Ladd, G.R. Beasley-Murray and others. Exegesis, biblical mega-themes, theology, philosophy and empirical historical realities all converge to provide sound reasons for retaining the pre-utopian framework. Pre-utopianism is certainly easier to reconcile with the postmodern situation than modernistic and triumphalistic utopianisms.

The abandonment of premillennialism is rather unrealistic at present, in the era of Israel's rebirth, Auschwitz and Hiroshima, the founding of Israel, recurring tensions and terrorism in the Middle East, the possible birth of the postmodern era, and missiles falling on Israel and Lebanon. Premillennialism is a timely story for the twentieth century. It makes sense. It is even no surprise that eschatomania seems to make sense in our atomic and manic era. Hence, evangelical scholars of various eschatological schools who are concerned about social justice should be interested in seeing the premillennial vision modified and purged of its anti-intellectual and anti-cultural accretions. Even for those who remain unconvinced of the truth of pre-utopianism, it may be acknowledged that there is a common eschatological ground of intellectual vitality and cultural engagement broad enough to encompass all millennial perspectives. In particular, Shrewd Utopianism, Earthy Non-Utopianism and a modified Pre-Utopianism could share in some basic socio-eschatological convictions.

A second option—for those wanting to scandalize pre-utopian

apathy relative to race relations or a host of issues—is to criticize the overly zealous forms of speculative and pessimistic premillennialism; to "tone down" premillennialism. On the surface this de-emphasizing of eschatology seems appropriate but: 1) it has been attempted before with little apparent effect[51]; and 2) it may douse the zealous flames of the biblical and volatile *eschatological impulse* that could be utilized to motivate evangelicals to live biblically and animate intellectually and culturally. Rather than marginalize eschatology in order to avoid extremism, why not modify and centralize the eschatological outlook in a biblical and intellectually healthy fashion? Why not promote a biblical and premillennial story for fit minds and socially compassionate hearts? Premillennial lay persons need a compelling vision to direct their eschatological energies in a constructive fashion. Both colonial and nineteenth-century America witnessed orthodox believers engaging in intellectual pursuits and large-scale social programs, in part, because of the eschatological impulse.[52] Unfortunately, this utopianism was very vulnerable to cultural triumphalism (e.g., civil postmillennialism), racism and disillusionment. A modified premillennialism, however, could ground cultural and intellectual pursuits within a powerful eschatological orientation that seeks to approximate the millennium in the present and longs to experience the fulfillment of the present in the post-Parousia millennium of the future.

Hence, a broad distinction needs to be made between pre-utopian theologies. The *Naive Pre-Utopian* or anti-utopian tends to adopt an otherworldly, escapist, hermeneutically literalistic, pessimistic, fatalistic and last-generational orientation. He or she may be described as anti-utopian because he or she sees little or no theological and existential continuity between the present age and the Post-Parousia era. The millennium is basically irrelevant. He or she may be described as naive because he or she naively accepts a pessimistic interpretation of historical events and the flow of history. Lindseyism contributes greatly to anti-utopianism or naive pre-utopianism.

Incoherent Pre-Utopianism, very popular in America today, simultaneously embraces social transformation, even civil postmillennialism and Manifest Destiny, while also plotting the end of the world in this last generation. The salient dualism of the incoherentist, where the present darkness is spreading even while America is being saved, contributes to a triumphalistic or even militant social posture laced with motifs such as "take back," "take over," "redeem America" or "save our Christian nation."

Approximational Pre-Utopianism is shrewdly optimistic but not utopian about the possibility of positive change in the Church and society prior to the Lord's return. Some aspects of the coming utopia can be partially realized in the present, such as: a measure of international cooperation and social justice; reconciliation with God; reconciliation with others; some measure of racial reconciliation; cultural accomplishments like the creation of beautiful symphonies; intellectual breakthroughs in all academic disciplines; various experiences of enjoying God's good creation; and socially productive scientific discovery. This approximational paradigm or socio-eschatological model is surprised neither by Auschwitz *nor* the fall of the Berlin Wall, and preserves the zeal but not the naivete of nineteenth-century post-utopianism. Both the millennium and the hellish Great Tribulation can be approximated now, depending upon how man receives God's grace or utilizes the God-given talents of the *imago dei*. Approximationism avoids the naive optimism of the nineteenth-century and the despair and angst of the twentieth-century. Unlike modernism and utopianism, approximationism does not attempt prematurely and triumphalistically to force a unified vision of reality on humanity that obliterates the multiple stories of the human situation. All stories are not of equal value, however, when judged by the *telos*-story of a coming utopia. The coming utopia celebrates diversity (multiple nations and races), but prophetically critiques self-destructive values and stories such as racism or ethnic genocide. The theologically approximational church seeks to influence (a mild term) and occasionally transform (a strong term) the present by embodying the future in attitude, word and deed.

6. The Trajectories of Approximational Pre-Utopianism

Approximationism views the kingdom of God, a present rule with a future concretized global manifestation, as a central eschato-biblical concept, and the central teaching of the King. The biblical doctrines of the creation, incarnation and consummation are unified in the kingdom concept, as are soteriology and ethics. Stanley Hauerwas has noted that a century of biblical scholarship has established the fact that New Testament ethics is eschatological.[53] This means that the solution to racial strife is eschatological; racial healing in the Church is an eschatological event that can radiate throughout society.

Approximationism replaces pretribulational escapism with posttribulational social responsibility. It replaces a pessimistic or incoherent social posture with a confidence in the ability of the Church to influence and sometimes to transform the course of history. Approximationism synthesizes the zeal and optimism of postmillennialism, the historical realism of amillennialism, and the contemporary premillennial awareness of the reality of sin and the power of Antichrist. Fatalistic historical determinism is repudiated and the fluidity and plasticity of the historical drama is affirmed. The kingdom is not solely future, for D-day, Christ's death, burial and resurrection, has triumphed over the present darkness. The promising light of the future may be conditionally brought to bear on the present, contingent upon the human response to grace. Speculative date-setting and last-generationism are abandoned in favor of an any-generation mentality that takes seriously the possibility of long-term social responsibility and planning. The Church is committed to history for the duration. Rapture-escapism and Platonic or Gnostic otherworldliness is orphaned and a Hebraic commitment to God's good creation is adopted. Tribulations such as the horrors of the twentieth century may result, in part, from apathetic ghetto Christianity rather than from a divinely determined plan. A selective hermeneutical literalism is deemed prejudicial and inadequate, and a consistent hermeneutic which emphasizes the kingdom teaching of Jesus is affirmed. When selective literalism is abandoned, the premillennial Church begins to recognize that the cosmos may be quite ancient and that God does things slowly.[54] Hence, for many reasons, pre-utopians can conceptualize long-term programs of social amelioration. Fast-food racial reconciliation and integration suffer from a spiritual malnutrition that will eventually create other social pathologies.

Approximationism avoids both triumphalism and separatism. It avoids both naive utopianism and cynical pessimism. It is, fundamentally, a shrewd expression of neighbor-love.

The present premillennial understanding of the purpose of eschatology often is as follows: it serves as ammunition for opportunistic, lifeboat evangelism; or it serves as a means for personal assurance in bewildering times; or it serves as a means for the opportunistic marketing of books that plot the end of the world. In contrast, approximationism views eschatology as a call to change and abandon idolatries such as racism. The purpose of biblical eschatology is not merely to understand, predict and interpret the future, in various ways; the point of eschatology is to change the present in the Presence of the future.

7. The Practical Application of Approximational Racial Reconciliation

The Church should be viewed as an eschatological community that proclaims, celebrates, models, anticipates and mediates the millennial *telos* of racial unity in an approximational fashion. Some practical applications of approximationism to the issue of racial reconciliation would at least include the following:

1) The premillennial Church would undergo an eschatological reorientation or revision that directs the eschatological impulse out of the saltshaker and into the world. Premillennialism needs a future-vision that ignites its commitment to social melioration in general and racial reconciliation in particular.

2) The writing, teaching, publishing and purchasing of Lindseyan books should be discouraged. Authors and publishers have a moral responsibility.

3) The goal of immediate total integration in the Church and society would be viewed as naively utopian,[55] while the separate-but-equal approach would be considered as a static, status-quo realism that has lost the utopian edge and the dynamic eschatological viewpoint. A policy that constantly moves forward by pursuing some measure of integration in society while realistically acknowledging separate and equal racial realities would be consistent with approximationism. Pastors should both celebrate and model eschatological racial unity via numberless creative activities. These types of reconciliatory opportunities send a powerful message to a racist society.

4) Churches should clearly condemn overt and covert racism, and make it clear that racists will not inherit the kingdom of God now or ever. When racial tensions flare up in society pastors must proclaim the truth.

5) Dispensationalism's self-reform effort, known as Progressive Dispensationalism, has transcended many of the socially debilitating tendencies of its more traditional and Darbyist predecessors. It could develop a comprehensive eschatological social ethic. A progressive and renewed Dallas[56] should bring about a Copernican revolution in the socio-eschatological orbit of countless evangelical pastors and laypersons. The transformation of dispensationalism could foreshadow the transformation of evangelical social ethics, for traditional Darbyism is truly a major obstacle to constructive change. However, as mentioned previously, not only must the excesses of Lindseyism be criticized and abandoned, but the power and constructive social relevance of premillennial eschatology must be rediscovered. It is not enough to criticize and tone down eschatology. Eschatology should be emphasized with a Lindseyan fervor but without Lindseyan theological errors. In one sense Lindsey was right: eschatology is relevant to every historical situation.

6) The writings of Jurgen Moltmann and other hopeful theologians have made an enormous contribution to the discussion of the relation between eschatology and social concern. Their shrewd utopianism and panentheistic metaphysic should not be

accepted uncritically, yet the Theology of Hope can serve as a helpful resource for reflection upon social issues such as racism.

7) The writings and stories of heroic believers who have caught the eschatological vision of transcending racism should be read and discussed in our colleges and churches. Many of these works are completely unknown to contemporary evangelicals.

8) Worship and hymnody in the local church must do more than cater to a spiritual sensualism. Reflection and meditation upon the blessings of God, the emphasizing of ways to overcome personal problems in sermon and lesson, and experiencing the powerful presence of God in praise—all of which are valuable if biblical and theologically sound—are theologically suspect if praxis does not result. It would be neither easy nor simple, but eschato-praxis could be included as a goal of true worship and praise. Hymns and songs that encourage (or implicitly justify) believers who disengage from serving God in this world should be replaced with biblical alternatives. The superficiality of much evangelical worship and preaching may be at least partially attributable to the current eschatological climate.

9) The implications of the theology of the millennium need to be explored and heralded. A recognition that this earth, including culture, politics, international relations, the academy and the arts, will be transformed in the coming age counters separatism, Platonic and Gnostic otherworldliness, pessimism and escapism. The millennial *telos*, where all races are united in worship and service of the Lion of Judah, also judges the present sinful reality of racism.

10) Biblical social praxis should be viewed as a secondary test of the truthfulness of eschatological pronouncements and formulations. Any eschatological system which logically entails social inertia and a neglect of the countless biblical admonitions requiring social justice needs to be reformulated or rejected.[57] Nevertheless, Ramesh Paul Richard openly repudiates the criterion of praxis:

> It is assumed that an eschatology which is optimistic and motivates action is better than that which is not. How-

ever, those are false criteria. One must find out which eschatology derives from the Bible even though it may be less activistic and optimistic in effect. Perhaps this would provide the checks and balances needed to keep Christians involved without trusting themselves.[58]

Regrettably, Richard overlooks the fundamental criticism that any eschatological system which is logically irreconcilable with the numerous biblical commands to "let justice roll on like a river" (Amos 5:24) not only fails the pragmatic test but is biblically suspect and theologically impoverished. Carl F.H. Henry correctly argues that any view of the future that undermines the "world-relevance" of the gospel is less than biblical. "Whatever in our kingdom views undercuts that relevance," he concludes, "destroys the essential character of Christianity as such."[59] Richard's rejection of the criterion of praxis seems to be rooted in the overwhelming belief that "premillennialism is pessimistic" about the future prior to the Lord's return.[60] A more helpful and biblical approach would be to view praxis as a secondary test of theology. The primary test is fidelity to Scripture, but Scripture itself views orthodoxy and orthopraxy as overlapping entities.[61] This discussion of the criterion of praxis leads to a final consideration.

11) The Church has solid biblical and empirical reasons for proclaiming hope for this present racist age prior to Christ's return. Postmillennialism may have overstated its case, but it is rather arrogant not to recognize the persuasiveness of the great postmillennial theologians and biblical scholars when they claim that there is a biblical foundation for affirming that the kingdom rule of God is spreading (like leaven) throughout God's world. God's rule has already arrived. Additionally, empirical evidence suggests that the future has indeed made a great difference at various times in this age. Consider the following results of D-day: infanticide and abortion largely disappeared in the Roman Empire; the gladiatorial games ceased in the Roman Empire; widespread acceptance of homosexuality by the cultural elite and widespread homosexual practices essen-

tially vanished in the Roman Empire; beautiful symphonies and art forms were created for the glory of God; scientific invention, discovery and medical breakthroughs resulted as scholars sought to study God's second great book, the creation, and think God's thoughts after Him; slavery was abolished on multiple continents by the inspiration of revivalists; imperfect political theories and imperfect nations were formed that were much more perfect than previous forms, due to Christian influence on the newer forms; countless social betterment programs and educational institutions were founded as a means to serve the Savior; and even this present bloody century has witnessed heroes of the faith who have opposed dictators or racism as they carried their crosses for the King of the kingdom. The biblically and empirically based message that can and should be proclaimed from every evangelical pulpit is that, because of D-day, the Church can make a difference—even in an era of racism and burning churches.[62] This kingdom message has propelled masses of evangelicals out of the pews and into the worldwide parish in the past, and it can happen again—provided that last-generationism, fatalism and escapism are replaced with an explosive eschatological vision for this age.[63]

Those who will "reign with" Christ (2 Timothy 2:12; Revelation 20:6) in the coming international and earthly utopia have the superlative rationale for social, cultural and intellectual pursuits. Such pursuits bring the rule of God to the present (the already) and are preparatory for the future (the not yet). This tension between the present and the future guards against two dangerous cultural postures: 1) separatism—because the transformed world *is* our home; and 2) theocratic triumphalism—because premillennial anthropology realistically reminds us of our own sinfulness, and because premillennial eschatology teaches us that the not yet remains. The assumptions of Darbyism have contributed to both errors.

While triumphalistic and eschatologically incoherent evangelicals undermine their own worthy goal of returning moral decency to education and public life by indecently offending everyone, urban centers lose all hope, indecency spreads unchecked and both academic and popular cultures putrefy. While the premillennial Church literalistically speculates about the end of the world, many inner-city children see their world literally come to an end. While the eschatomaniacs debate the tribulation, millions live amidst great and insufferable tribulation. While thousands of economically comfortable evangelicals respond to the darkness by hopefully waiting for the rapture, the malnourished lose all hope waiting for their daily bread. While pastors thrill their audiences with stories of nuclear bombs burning the earth with fire, black churches literally burn to the ground.

Ronald C. Potter warns the Church as follows:

> If our gospel cannot deal with the issues of violent crime—moral and spiritual disentegration—drugs, AIDS, unwed juvenile parenthood—and the spirit of hopelessness and despair in our communities, then this gospel is irrelevant and powerless and deserves to be replaced by something like Islam.[64]

Those seeking hope for this present age often feel that they either have to abandon God and biblical orthodoxy, or retain premillennialism and abandon hope for social melioration prior to Christ's return. Approximationism avoids this false dilemma and proclaims and actualizes a gospel which is realistic, optimistic and relevant for this age and the age to come.

Conclusion

It has been argued that the gospel of the kingdom of Jesus includes the ultimate earthly hope and reality of the millennium and the penultimate earthly hope and reality of the approximational presence of the future now. Jesus came proclaiming a global rule and coming kingdom. He did not speak of the future or the presence of the future to ease human curiosity or merely supply a theological sedative. He demanded repentance and fruit. He called for change. His already-initiated reign is a global reign with a future global manifestation. He spoke of and embodied the future in order to transform the present and future of the entire cosmos. If the Church follows in His steps it will avoid stumbling into the next millennium and His gospel will not be deemed irrelevant to any social issue, including racism.

The premillennial, evangelical Church lacks a coherent utopian vision with both a this-worldly relevance and a strong dose of historical and anthropological realism. Utopian future-visions have led the charge on the battlefield, elicited heroic sacrifices and martyrdoms, dethroned powerful rulers and elevated new civilizations. Future-visions partially create the future. A coherent, realistic, praxis-provoking vision is the key to effective evangelical mission and witness in the next millennium. Evangelicals need a utopian *telos*.

Approximationism seeks to mitigate the intellectually and culturally debilitating effects of pathological premillennialism, excite and animate the pre-utopian social conscience, and provide a realistic yet optimistic interpretation of the present age. The self-definition of the approximational Christian is a fallen creature intended for earthly existence, cultural life and participation in ongoing growth and global renewal. By God's grace the passionate, visionary, praxis-oriented, worldly,[65] intellectually and culturally engaged Christian can impact the world. It is hoped that approximational pre-utopianism will contribute to the evangelical intellectual renaissance, the premillennial eschatological revolution and widespread racial eschato-reconciliation.

Endnotes

[1] The tragedy at Ruby Ridge illustrates how pathological eschatology and racism can be synthesized. The situation with the Freemen and the Waco tragedy reveal how the impact of certain views of the future may be increasing as we approach a new millennium. Many well-known evangelicals, such as Hal Lindsey, have popularized the view that the rebirth of Israel in 1948 or the retaking of Jerusalem in 1967 herald the beginning of the last generation (usually viewed as 40-100 years) of history. Persecution, the rapture, Great Tribulation and the Lord's return are imminent. Could Lindseyan evangelicalism have directly contributed to the distorted mentality of extremist groups? This question might warrant a scholarly study.

[2] For evidence of the widespread influence of these "demons," see below.

[3] George R. Beasley-Murray, *Jesus and the Kingdom of God* (Grand Rapids, MI: Eerdmans, 1986); George Eldon Ladd, *The Presence of the Future: The Eschatology of Biblical Realism* (Grand Rapids, MI: Eerdmans, 1974); Oscar Cullman, *Salvation in History*, trans. Sidney G. Sowers and SCM Press (New York: Harper and Row, 1967).

[4] Walter Rauschenbusch, *A Theology for the Social Gospel* (New York: MacMillan, 1917), 224.

[5] Ibid.

[6] *Eschatopraxis* is a concept borrowed from Carl E. Braaten, *Eschatology and Ethics: Essays on the Theology and Ethics of the Kingdom of God* (Minneapolis, MN: Augsburg, 1974), 110-11. It means conduct appropriate for the end times.

[7] Consider these prevalent evangelical attitudes as expressed in popular hymns: "His chosen ones shall gather to their home beyond the skies"; "When all of life is over and our work on earth is done"; "Then to heaven we'll fly away"; "In the sweet by and by, we shall meet on that beautiful shore"; "I'm not discouraged, I'm heaven bound"; "Face to face I shall behold Him, Far beyond the starry sky"; "I am weary, O so weary of trav'ling here below"; "I am bound for the promised land"; "This troubled world is not my final home"; "The soul of man is like a waiting falcon—When it's released, it's destined for the skies"; "Someday we'll leave this world of sin With all its dark despair;" "And we can worship at His feet Beyond the stars above"; "I'll fly away." These songs contain partial truths but tend to obscure the biblical truth that Christ will return *to earth* and transform earthly existence. The Christian hope is not a Greek desire to flee earthly existence. Rather, the Christian hope is to overcome sin and see earthly existence transformed into utopia. The transformed world truly is our home.

[8] Jurgen Moltmann, "Politics and the Practice of Hope," *The Christian Century* 87 (11 March 1970): 289.

[9] Martin Luther King, Jr., "I Have a Dream," in *A Documentary History of Religion in America: Since 1865*, ed. Edwin S. Gaustad (Grand Rapids, MI: Eerdmans, 1983), 496-97. Objections to King's vision will be considered briefly. In short, those who fail to appreciate his accomplishments have historical amnesia. Likewise, those who fail to recognize how much still needs to be accomplished are living in a dream world.

[10] See footnote #14 for a discussion of the proper definition of evangelicalism.

[11] Harriet Beecher Stowe, *Uncle Tom's Cabin* (New York: Collier Books, A Division of Macmillan Publishing Co., 1962), 510-11.

12 Timothy L. Smith, *Revivalism and Social Reform: American Protestantism on the Eve of the Civil War* (Baltimore: John Hopkins University Press, 1980); Donald W. Dayton, *Discovering Our Evangelical Heritage* (New York: Harper and Row, 1976).

13 How this standard applies to sins of ignorance or omission is less clear, and perhaps terrifying.

14 The attempt to define "evangelicalism" or "American evangelicalism" has been plagued with controversy, but regardless of the value of the label, there does appear to be a loose movement of Christians in America today that are partially and historically descended from early twentieth-century American fundamentalists. They share, for the most part, common convictions concerning evangelism, personal conversion and acceptance of Christ as Savior, crucientrism, biblical authority, major Christian doctrines such as the deity of Christ and a general Trinitarian orientation, supernaturalism, some aspects of personal piety and devotion and a renunciation of some of the errors of hyper-fundamentalism. See: Timothy P. Weber, "Premillennialism and the Branches of Evangelicalism," in *The Variety of Evangelicalism*, eds. Donald Dayton and Robert K. Johnston (Downers Grove, IL: InterVarsity Press, 1991); Alister McGrath, *Evangelicalism and the Future of Christianity* (Downers Grove, IL: InterVarsity Press, 1995), 55-87; Mark A. Noll, *The Scandal of the Evangelical Mind* (Grand Rapids, MI: Eerdmans, 1994), 7-10; James Leo Garrett, Jr., E. Glenn Hinson and James E. Tully, *Are Southern Baptists Evangelicals?* (Macon, GA: Mercer University Press, 1983); and James Alden Hedstrom, "Evangelical Program in the United States, 1945-1980: The Morphology of Establishment, Progressive, and Radical Platforms" (Ph.D. diss., Vanderbilt University, 1982). Also see John G. Stackhouse, Jr., "Evangelical Cornucopia," *Christianity Today* 35 (25 November 1991): 31, for reviews of Dayton, *Variety*, and a work by George M. Marsden, *Understanding Fundamentalism and Evangelicalism* (published by Eerdmans).

15 Shirley C. Guthrie, "Human Suffering, Human Liberation, and the Sovereignty of God," *Theology Today* 53 (April 1996): 22-34.

16 This is not a suggestion to uncritically embrace panentheism or the open view of God (Pinnock).

17 Harold Hoehner, interviewed by Randy Frame, in "Is Christ or Satan Ruler of This World?" *Christianity Today* 34 (5 March 1990): 42-44.

18 The italicized and capitalized titles in this paragraph are, with one exception (the last book listed), from contemporary eschatological works such as: Frank E. Peretti, *This Present Darkness* (Westchester, IL: Crossway Books, 1986). Christian bookstores carry many of these types of works.

19 D. L. Moody, "The Return of the Lord" [1877], in *The American Evangelicals, 1800-1900: An Anthology*, ed. William G. McLoughlin (New York: Harper and Row, 1968), 185.

20 Os Guiness, *Fit Bodies, Fat Minds: Why Evangelicals Don't Think and What to Do About It* (Grand Rapids, MI: Baker Books, 1994), 38.

21 Proving that the Bible is true because it predicted the present darkness, international troubles, problems in the Middle East, the invention of Cobra helicopters or the atomic bomb, etc.

22 Issac C. Rottenberg, *The Promise and the Presence: Toward a Theology of the Kingdom of God* (Grand Rapids, MI: Eerdmans, 1980), 48. If I tried to convince a Christian publisher that I had written a book that describes a Christian way to predict the winning number in a multi-million Powerball lottery, I suspect that the publishers would refuse to print such nonsense, even if such a book might be a best-seller. Given 2,000 years of false predictions claiming that we are in the last generation, one wonders what it will take for Christian publishers to become cognizant of the harm and folly of these works. Lindseyism not only numbs the social conscience and clouds the mind of the evangelical Church, but it also contributes to the immediatism and widespread social irresponsibility of our present age.

23 Millard Erickson, *Contemporary Options in Eschatology: A Study of the Millennium* (Grand Rapids, MI: Baker Book House, 1977), 160. Eschatomania refers to an intensive preoccupation with the prophetic passages or details of the Bible, eschatological charts, prophecy studies, end-times predictions and preaching, etc. See Millard Erickson, *Christian Theology* (Grand Rapids, MI: Baker Book House, 1985), 1152.

24 Noll, *Scandal*. Guiness, *Fit Bodies*. Both authors recognize the value of some of these features of evangelicalism when not distorted.

25 Rottenberg, *The Promise and the Presence*, 48.

26 Vernon Grounds, *Evangelism and Social Responsibility* (Scottdale, PA: Herald Press, 1969), 6.

27 An introductory discussion of whether premillennialism entails social inertia can be found below.

28 In this work, the terms "mind," "head," "heart" and "hand" will be used frequently. "Mind" and "head" are used synonymously and refer to the aspect of evangelical life addressed in the works by Noll and Guiness: the intellectual realm, thinking, analysis, creative intellectual construction, etc. These terms, "head," "heart" and "hand," are not being used identically with their biblical meanings. Instead, "head" refers to the intellectual or academic. "Heart" refers to the emotional, the feelings, the passions and attitudes, the psychological and the moral character of a person. "Hand" refers to actions, deeds, good works and social action. These definitions are more in keeping with contemporary usage.

29 Weber, "Premillennialism and the Branches," 5.

30 Hal Lindsey, *The Late Great Planet Earth* (Grand Rapids: Zondervan, 1970).

Tom Sine, "Bringing Down the Final Curtain: Doomsday Predictions and the God of History," *Sojourners*, June-July 1984, 10.

31 Yehezkel Landau, "The President and the Prophets: Balancing Biblical Warnings and Promises," *Sojourners*, June-July 1984, 24. Also see: Timothy Weber, *Living in the Shadow of the Second Coming: American Premillennialism, 1875-1982* (Chicago: University of Chicago Press, 1987), viii.; and Stephen O'Leary and Michael McFarland, "The Political Use of Mythic Discourse: Prophetic Interpretation in Pat Robertson's Presidential Campaign," *Quarterly Journal of Speech* 75 (November 1989): 450, for documentation of the flurry of media articles relative to Reagan's eschatology and public policy.

32 Weber, "Premillennialism and the Branches," 5, and Weber, *Living in the Shadow*, 32-33.

33 George Marsden, *Reforming Fundamentalism: Fuller Seminary and the New Evangelicalism* (Grand Rapids, MI: Eerdmans, 1984), 305. Christianity Today Institute, "Our Future Hope: Eschatology and Its Role in the Church," *Christianity Today* 31 (6 February 1987): 9 (I).

34 Paul Boyer, *When Time Shall Be No More: Prophecy Belief in Modern American Culture* (Cambridge: Harvard University Press, 1992).

35 Traditional premillennialism's social posture is often an anti-utopian form of pre-utopianism. The pessimistic, escapist, last-generational premillennialist might be best described as anti-utopian, for the millennium is basically irrelevant to the present, other than serving as some kind of ambiguous reward.

36 Edgar Whisenant, *On Borrowed Time* and *88 Reasons Why the Rapture Will Be in 1988*, Two Books in One (Nashville: World Bible Society), 1988.

37 These stories, while partially fictional, are all based upon socio-eschatological comments made by real people who have been encountered by the author.

38 Brook Noel Moore and Kenneth Bruder, *The Power of Ideas* (Mountain View, CA: Mayfield Publishing Co., 1990), 1.

39 Oscar Cullman writes:

> The decisive battle has already been won. But the war continues until a certain, though not as yet definite, Victory Day when the weapons will at last be still. The decisive battle would be Christ's death and resurrection, and Victory Day his *parousia*. Between the two lies a short but *important* span of time already indicating a fulfilment [*sic*] and an anticipation of peace, in which, however, the greatest watchfulness is demanded. Yet it is from the decisive battle now won and the Victory Day yet to be achieved that this span of time gets its meaning and its demands.

Cullman, *Salvation in History*, trans., Sidney G. Sowers and SCM Press

103

(New York: Harper and Row, 1967), 44.

[40] This task also goes beyond the limitations of this present study, but see below, and see Douglas K. Matthews, "Approximating the Millennium: Toward a Coherent Premillennial Theology of Social Transformation." Ph.D. diss., Baylor University, 1992.

[41] See Randy Frame, "End-times Prediction Draws Strong Following," *Christianity Today* 38 (20 June 1994): 46-47.

[42] Rodney Clapp, "Overdosing on the Apocalypse: How End-Times Junkies Can Become Sane and Responsible," *Christianity Today* 35 (28 October 1991): 26-29.

[43] See below, and see Matthews, "Approximating."

[44] Guiness, *Fit Bodies*, 63.

[45] Erickson, *Contemporary Options*, 160.

[46] John D. Woodbridge, Mark A. Noll and Nathan O. Hatch, *The Gospel in America: Themes in the Story of America's Evangelicals* (Grand Rapids, MI: Zondervan, 1979), 240-41; Weber, *Living*, 74-78; Dayton, *Evangelical Heritage*, 113, 127, 145-46; Norris Magnuson, *Salvation in the Slums: Evangelical Social Work, 1865-1920*, ATLA Monograph Series, no. 10 (Metuchen, NJ: The Scarecrow Press and The American Theological Library Association, 1977), 17; David O. Moberg, *The Great Reversal: Evangelism versus Social Action* (Philadelphia: J.B. Lippincott Co., 1972), 38; and David A. Rausch, "Premillennialism and Social Concern, 1865-1940: A Comparison with Historical Trends in Protestantism in the United States," in *The Return of the Millennium*, eds. Joseph Bettis and S.K. Johannesen (New York: International Religious Foundation, Inc., 1984).

[47] Martin E. Marty, *Protestantism in the United States: Righteous Empire*, 2nd ed. (New York: Charles Scribner's Sons, 1986), 248.

[48] John Walvoord, "Why Must Christ Return?" in *Prophecy and the Seventies*, ed. Charles Lee Feinberg (Chicago: Moody Press, 1971), 43.

[49] See Matthews, "Approximating," 57-92. *Antagonistic:* Attempts to improve the world are opposed because they might delay the Parousia, or corrupt the Church by involvement with the world or the liberal social gospel. An extremist variant of this view is survivalist (usually posttribulational) premillennialism, where believers retreat from the world and stockpile weapons and food in order to survive apocalyptic tribulations. *Symptomatic:* The world cannot be improved, but individuals need to be cared for, and/or individual physical aid might lead to personal salvation. *Preservative:* It might be possible to slow down the present decay or decline of society or a once-great America even though the end is near (there are coherent and incoherent subvarieties). *Transformational* (many strategic subvarieties): The world (culture, society) can be transformed significantly for the better. *Influential-*

Transformational: A milder form of the transformational view that is strategically eclectic and very cautious about the usage of transformationist language (avoids triumphalistic language such as "saving America," "saving our Christian nation," "taking over," "taking back," "changing or transforming the world," etc.). The argument that these distinctions are insignificant relative to premillennial social concern is flawed.

50 Alva J. McClain, "A Premillennial Philosophy of History," *Bibliotheca Sacra* 113 (April 1956): 113-14.

51 A visit to a local Christian bookstore and perusal of best-selling book titles suggests that eschatomania continues to rule in evangelicalism in spite of criticisms of this phenomenon by scholars such as Millard Erickson (see above) or works such as C. Marvin Pate and Calvin B. Haines, *Doomsday Delusions: What's Wrong with Predictions about the End of the World* (Downers Grove, IL: InterVarsity Press, 1995).

52 See above.

53 Stanley Hauerwas and William H. Willimon, *Resident Aliens: A Provocative Assessment of Culture and Ministry for People Who Know That Something Is Wrong* (Nashville, TN: Abingdon Press, 1989), 86-87.

54 Richard J. Mouw, "Humility, Hope and the Divine Slowness," *The Christian Century* 107 (11 April 1990): 365.

55 See the comments concerning integration and utopianism by Eugene Rivers in "Separate and Equal," by Wendy Murray Zoba, *Christianity Today* 40 (5 February 1996): 14-24.

56 Here "Dallas" serves as a symbol of the center of dispensationalism. Obviously, key traditionalists and progressives serve at other institutions.

57 Much more needs to be said here and some terms need to be defined. Space limitations make it impossible to adequately address this issue. See Matthews, "Approximating," 103-109.

58 Ramesh Paul Richard, "Hermeneutical Prolegomena to a Premillennial Social Ethics" (Th.D. diss., Dallas Theological Seminary, 1982), 299.

59 Carl F.H. Henry, *The Uneasy Conscience of Modern Fundamentalism* (Grand Rapids, MI: Eerdmans, 1947), 53.

60 Richard, "Hermeneutical Prolegomena," 270.

61 Consider the Pauline and synoptic teachings on faith (intellectual assent and personal trust) and works, or the simultaneous demand in both Jesus' and Paul's ministry for correct belief and action. Knowing the truth and living the truth should be inseparable.

62 Believers are to be faithful regardless of results, but it is biblically and empirically justifiable to be hopeful and concerned about results. It is also rather silly to simultaneously issue calls for action while proclaiming that

results do not matter and that the world is hopelessly shipwrecked.

63 Utopianism is not needed to motivate believers to live sacrificially. Millions (even unbelievers) have given their lives throughout history (consider World War II) in the attempt to preserve or create a decent but non-utopian existence, or to oppose tyranny. The goal of perfection is not required to produce praxis. However, fatalism and pessimism clearly undermine coherent large-scale social reform efforts.

64 Ronald C. Potter, "Responding to Farrakhan," *Urban Family*, Spring 1996, 7.

65 Not worldly in the sense of being conformed to rebellious world systems or practices, but worldly in the incarnational sense. Christians are to participate fully in the life of the world, just as Christ did, even to the point of public death on a cross. It is often the case that only the way of the cross can mediate the appropriate presence of the future now.

Holy Laughter and Other Phenomena in Evangelical and Holiness Revival Movements

Paul L. King

With the phenomena associated with the "Toronto Blessing" and the ministry of Rodney Howard-Browne, people have tended to either completely accept or completely reject all such phenomena. Many of these manifestations have occurred in evangelical and holiness revival movements. When we look at the history of the Church, in particular the holiness movements which are akin to the beginnings of The Christian and Missionary Alliance, we see that such phenomena were neither accepted out of hand, nor dismissed summarily. As one of our Alliance writers, T.J. McCrossan, put it, regarding supernatural manifestations we should take "the middle of the road."[1] This study explores the experiences of evangelical and holiness revivals, including those of The Christian and Missionary Alliance, and how such manifestations were viewed.

Holy Laughter

Jonathan Edwards describes the reaction of some who were converted in the Great Awakening revival: "Their joyful surprise has caused their hearts as it were to leap, so that they have been ready to break forth into laughter, tearing often at the same time issuing like a flood, and intermingling a loud weeping."[2] E.M. Bounds records Wesley saying, "The power of God came mightily upon us, so that many cried out for exceeding joy, and many fell to the ground."[3] Charles Finney wrote that after he testified about his experience of being baptized in the Spirit, a normally serious elder of his church "fell into a most spasmodic laughter. It seemed as if it was impossible for him to keep from laughing from the very bottom of his heart."[4]

Manifestations of holy laughter and being drunk in the Spirit occurred during the Australian Keswick Convention of 1891:

> The Convention was marked by clean-cut surrender to God for all His will to be done at all costs, and by an overflowing joy which followed in hundreds of hearts, so that, as Mr. George Soltau wrote, "Literally 'our mouths were filled with laughter and our tongues with singing.' . . . It was impossible to restrain one's heart, the Lord giving us such a foretaste of heaven. Talk of 'fleshly excitement,' I wish to bear my testimony that it was nothing less than the fullness of the Spirit. We were verily drunk with the joy of the Lord, and with the vistas of the possibilities of faith opening up to the fully surrendered life of the believer. But it was equally manifest to us all that this joy and blessing is only to be received and retained and increased by the death *to* self and *of* self and the most painful crucifixion of self." [5]

In 1897 A.B. Simpson wrote that one of the effects of being filled with the Spirit is "fullness of Joy so that the heart is constantly radiant. This does not depend on circumstances, but fills the spirit with holy laughter in the midst of the most trying surroundings."[6]

Oswald Chambers recorded in his diary on April 19, 1907:

> Last night we had a blessed time. I was called down by the teachers to pray and anoint a lady who wanted healing, and as we were doing it God came so near that upon my word we were laughing as well as praying! How ut-

terly stilted we are in our approach to God. Oh that we lived more up to the light of all our glorious privileges.[7]

Again Chambers records in his journal May 6, 1907, "It is an unspeakably blessed thing to see souls come out under the blessing of the baptism of the Holy Ghost and Fire. Some simply laugh, peals of the heartiest and most blessed laughter you ever heard, just a modern edition of 'Then was our mouth filled with laughter.' "[8] A third time Chambers writes on May 27, "Many souls cut loose, there were tears and laughter and all the blessed signs of those revival times the Lord brings so mysteriously and suddenly upon His people. It is a great business to open up all the windows of the soul to heaven and live on the Hallelujah side."[9] Chambers evidently believed that laughter could be one of the signs of revival and, like Simpson, a result of the baptism in the Spirit.

Praying John Hyde, the great intercessor and missionary to China, also experienced holy laughter in the summer of the same year. His companion relates of a low caste Punjabi intercessor:

How often has G____, after most awful crying seemed to break through the hosts of evil and soar up into the presence of the Father! You could see the smile of God reflected in his face. Then he would laugh aloud in the midst of his prayer. It was the joy of a son revelling in the delight of his father's smile. God has been teaching John [Hyde] and me that his name is the God of Isaac— laughter. . . . Rejoicing, laughing, the same word as Isaac. This holy laughter seemed to relieve the tension and give Heaven's own refreshment to wrestling spirits.[10]

Sometimes related to the laughing phenomenon is a spontaneous dancing for joy. Praying Hyde, a staid Presbyterian, is described after a time of intense prayer at the Sialkot Convention (similar to Keswick), "He begins to sing, ' 'Tis done, the great transaction's done,' and he is so full of joy that his whole body begins to move, he claps his hands, then his feet begin to move, and look! he begins to dance for joy, and others join him until the whole place rings with God's praises."[11]

A.W. Tozer also testified of holy laughter:

> Now I say that worship is subject to degrees of perfection and intensity. There have been those who worshiped God to the place where they were in ecstasies of worship. I once saw a man kneel at an altar, taking Communion. Suddenly he broke into holy laughter. This man laughed until he wrapped his arms around himself as if he was afraid he would bust just out of sheer delight in the presence of Almighty God. . . . So worship is capable of running from the very simple to the most intense and sublime.[12]

Nevertheless, we must recognize that some laughter *is* "fleshly excitement" and some may even be demonically inspired. Catholic exorcists have discerned that the devil may cause laughter to distract and disrupt.[13] In 1912, Evan Roberts and Jessie Penn-Lewis in their book *War on the Saints* also write of demonical inspired laughter with twisting and jerking.[14] John and Charles Wesley also recognized that some manifestations were unholy laughter.[15]

Falling Under the Power of the Spirit

As cited above, both Wesley and E.M. Bounds recognized falling to the ground as a manifestation from God. George Whitefield criticized Wesley for allowing the phenomenon until it began happening in his own meetings.[16] Jonathan Edwards indicated that a person may "fail bodily strength" due to fear of hell and the conviction of the Holy Spirit or due to a "foretaste of heaven."[17] Finney's ministry also frequently manifested what he called "falling under the power of God."[18] R.A. Torrey testifies of people falling under the power of God due to conviction of sin.[19] Presbyterian Jonathan Goforth makes reference to the phenomenon in his book *By My Spirit*, originally published by The Christian and Missionary Alliance.[20]

Instances of falling under the power of the Spirit also oc-
curred at Alliance meetings in 1907, including Simpson's Gos-
pel Tabernacle[21] and at Fred F. Bosworth's Christian and
Missionary Alliance church in Dallas in 1912.[22] Greek professor
T.J. McCrossan, who wrote the book *Speaking in Other Tongues:
Sign or Gift, Which?* published by The Christian and Missionary
Alliance in 1927, three years later wrote in another book, *Bodily
Healing and the Atonement*:

> Hundreds are healed, who do not fall under this power,
> because they simply trust God's promises; and it is the
> prayer of faith that heals. Going under this power seems,
> however, to bring an extra spiritual blessing. . . . This
> power is not hypnotism. . . . This is not devil power.[23]

McCrossan is cautious in his writings about accepting all supernatural manifestations, but he speaks positively about this one
in particular. This is because McCrossan is speaking out of the
experience of his own life, for he fell under God's power and
was enraptured with visions when he was baptized in the Spirit
in 1921.[24]

Physical Sensations

Such manifestations were sometimes accompanied by unusual
bodily sensations. Charles Finney avowed his baptism in the
Spirit was "like a wave of electricity, going through and through
me."[25] McCrossan wrote of a woman who received the baptism in
the Spirit: "The third one was filled, and for days there seemed to
be a veritable fire burning within her."[26] Early Alliance pastor
Dr. E.D. Whiteside's testimony of healing in 1888 included both
physical sensations and falling under the power of the Spirit:

> Like a flash of electricity, I was instantly thrilled. Every
> point of my body and nerves was controlled by a strange
> sensation that increased in volume, until I bowed lower
> and lower to the floor. I was filled with the ecstatic thrill.
> My physical frame was unable to stand the strain.[27]

111

Reminiscent of holy laughter, he reported that he felt he was on the verge of "dying from overjoy."[28]

Trembling, Shaking and Convulsions

At the outset of the Welsh revival of 1904, Evan Roberts experienced the phenomenon of shaking on several occasions:

> In the spring of 1904, Evan found himself, as it were, on the Mount of Transfiguration. In his own home and out on the countryside, his loving Heavenly Father revealed Himself to His child in an amazing overwhelming manner which filled his soul with divine awe. At these special seasons, every member of his body trembled until the bed was shaken.[29]

A more intense form of trembling or shaking is a convulsing of the body in contortions, characteristic of some under intense conviction. Jonathan Edwards described a child in this condition, "She continued crying, and writhing her body to and fro, like one in anguish of spirit."[30] Speaking of the revival of 1740-1742, Edwards writes, "It was a very frequent thing to see a house full of outcries, faintings, convulsions, and such like, both with distress, and also with admiration and joy."[31] These phenomena also occurred in the ministries of Finney and Wesley.[32] In some cases these were regarded as the work of the Holy Spirit, others of the flesh, and still others as demonic in origin.[33]

Strange Sounds and Behavior

Sometimes strange sounds accompanied some of these manifestations, such as groaning or weeping. A companion of Praying Hyde relates of Hyde and the Punjab Prayer Convention of 1906 (similar to Keswick), "We began to pray, and suddenly the great burden of that soul was cast upon us, and the room was filled with sobs and cries for one whom most of us had never seen or heard of before. Strong men lay on the ground groaning in agony for that soul."[34]

On the other hand, not all strange sounds can automatically be accepted as a result of the Spirit's workings. Many animal-like sounds and behavior have been recognized throughout Church history as demonic.[35] Such exhibitions in the early Pentecostal movement were also often considered demonic. A.B. Simpson observed, "There have been many instances where [seeking for] the gift of tongues led the subjects and the audiences in to the wildest excesses and were accompanied with voices and actions more closely resembling wild animals than rational beings, impressing the unprejudiced observers that it was the work of the devil."[36] Pentecostal leader Charles Parham also described demonic manifestations of barking like a dog, braying like a donkey, crowing like a rooster and contortions and fits.[37] Woodworth-Etter admonished:

> "Try the spirits." In one of our meetings there was a colored woman who had a wonderful experience spiritually; that is the kind the devil gets after. One day she commenced to go about on her knees, twisting about like a serpent. God does not tell anyone to do that. She spoke in tongues; then she said, "I don't want to do it; I don't want to do it."
>
> Everyone knew it was not of God; and I said to her: "that is not God; the enemy has got hold of you."[38]

While we see from this overview that animal sounds and behavior have been viewed throughout Church history as predominately demonic in origin, that is not to say that in every instance animal-like sounds and behavior are demonic. They may be of the flesh, or they may be a response to something God is doing in a person—like the unutterable groanings of Romans 8:26-27. The phenomena may even be misinterpreted by observers. A colleague of this writer who is a researcher of the Campbellite/Christian church movement determined through his research on the 1800 Cane Ridge revival that what was reported by the media as "barking up a tree" and "treeing the devil" was, in reality, people under such conviction and emo-

113

tional distress that they were heaving and groaning in such a manner that it sounded like barking and all the while feeling faint so that they were holding themselves up against a tree.

A missionary friend in South Africa reported that on two separate occasions he observed two different pastors apparently roaring. Believing the phenomena to be demonic, he attempted to cast out demons without any response. When questioned about it, in both instances each pastor responded that he was crying out in words for the nations to repent, but the listeners only heard roaring. This could be a similar phenomenon to the incident when God the Father spoke to Jesus and some thought it thundered (John 12:28-29), or when Paul heard Jesus speak but others only heard a sound (Acts 22:9).

This calls for caution in automatically branding all such phenomena as demonic. There may be occasions in which sounds are made that are from the heart and soul which cannot be articulated clearly, which may fall under the category of "groans that words cannot express" (Romans 8:26). Nonetheless, the preponderance of evidence would indicate that the vast majority of such animal-like manifestations are either demonically inspired or originate in the flesh. Those which are demonic in nature may be satanic counterfeits meant to deceive, or they may be already existing demonic influences being exposed or brought to the surface by the moving of the Holy Spirit in revival, like a bird dog flushing out a pheasant.

Impressions, Prophecies, Visions and Dreams

Contrary to the beliefs of some modern authors, such as Gary Friezen, who has claimed impressions have no part in a believer's life,[39] impressions and supernatural revelation from God were experienced in holiness and evangelical revival movements. A.T. Pierson writes of George Müller, "Müller cultivated habits of life which made his whole nature more and more open to divine impression, and so his sense of God became more and more keen and constant."[40] Praying Hyde, it is recorded, "began to have visions of the glorified Christ as a Lamb on His throne—suffering such infinite pain for and with

114

His suffering Body on earth."[41] Torrey recalled that a man praying for revival in Australia saw a prophetic vision of crowds of people coming to hear Torrey speak.[42] Prophecies and visions were features of the Welsh revival.[43]

Such manifestations occurred in the early Christian and Missionary Alliance as well. In fact, the missions emphasis of The Christian and Missionary Alliance was established on Simpson's response to a vivid dream in which he awoke trembling.[44] In 1883 early Alliance leader John Cookman had an experience in which "The Lord appeared to him in a vision, and said, 'I am thy Healer, thy Sanctifier, thy Savior, and thy Lord.'"[45] Robert Jaffray experienced several dreams with strong impressions from the Lord.[46] C.H. Gootee recounts a healing service led by A.B. Simpson and Henry Wilson in which he received a miraculous healing. When Wilson anointed him with oil, he saw a vision of the blood of Jesus sprinkled on his breast and body.[47]

But such experiences were not accepted automatically among holiness leaders and some Pentecostals.[48] In 1898 when Carrie Judd Montgomery had been very ill, she testified at The Christian and Missionary Alliance convention of prophecies that she received from three women, two of which said she would die, one of which said she would recover: "The Lord spoke to her and told her that I would be raised up speedily and that I would be able to attend the Christian Alliance [now The Christian and Missionary Alliance] convention, which would take place in a few days. I was so very weak and ill that her prophecy seemed incredible, but praise God, it came true." Of the two other women she said: "Two Christian women thought they had it from the Lord that I was going to die. . . . How this shows us that we must not depend on impressions that do not harmonize with the word of God. . . . Dear readers, always stand firmly upon God's Word, and not upon the impressions of those around you."[49]

Classic evangelical and holiness leaders understood that God can lead by such impressions and revelations, but they needed to be tested.[50] Moravian leader Count Zinzendorf, who was open to supernatural movings of the Holy Spirit, witnessed a man falling into an "inspired fit, jerking and convulsing, and prophesying. Zinzendorf did not hesitate to reject the inspiration."[51] John Wesley's timeless counsel is:

> Do not hastily ascribe things to God. Do not easily suppose dreams, voices, impressions, visions, or revelations to be from God. They may be from Him. They may be from Nature. They may be from the devil. Therefore believe not every spirit, but "try the spirits whether they be from God."[52]

Evan Roberts and Jessie Penn-Lewis comment that "No one can with safety accept all the supernatural manifestations which accompany Revival, or believe all seeming 'Pentecostal power' to be of God."[53] They recognized that gifts of the Spirit such as prophecy, healing and tongues could be genuine or false, saying that counterfeit tongues were only a fraction of the counterfeit manifestations.[54] Again they warn: "Counterfeit manifestations of the Divine life in various ways now follow quickly; movements in the body, pleasant thrills, touches, a glow as of fire in different parts of the body, or sensations of cold, or shakings and tremblings, all of which are accepted as from God."[55] However, they did not dismiss all such manifestations as demonic, for Roberts himself experienced some of these manifestations authentically during the Welsh revival, and was by experience able to recognize the counterfeit.[56]

Conclusion

These are just a sampling of the occurrences of such manifestations in evangelical and holiness movements. Hank Hanegraaff claims these phenomena are indicators of counterfeit revival.[57] While some such phenomena clearly are counterfeit, in the light of these examples it would be more accurate to say that there are counterfeits in the midst of revival. In most every revival in Church history—Wesleyan, Great Awakening, Cane Ridge, Welsh Revival—there has been mixture. Where there is counterfeit, there must also be the genuine. Wesley warned of a twofold danger: 1) to regard them too much, as essential to revival, 2) to regard them too little, condemning them altogether.[58] The position of the Alliance and early holiness leaders was one of a "middle ground," as McCrossan suggests, one that neither accepts nor rejects such phenomena without further discernment. The viewpoint of Jonathan Edwards (which both critics like Hanegraaff and Toronto Blessing supporters seem to ignore) is perhaps the wisest counsel:

> A work is not to be judged of by any effects on the bodies of men; such as tears, trembling, groans, loud outcries, agonies of body, or the failing of bodily strength. The influence persons are under is not to be judged of one way or other by such effects on the body; and the reason is because the Scripture no where gives us any such rule. We cannot conclude that persons are under the influence of the true Spirit because we see such effects on their bodies, because this is not given as a mark of the true Spirit; nor on the other hand, have we any reason to conclude, from any such outward appearances, that persons are not under the influence of the Spirit of God, because there is no rule of Scripture given us to judge of spirits by, that does neither expressly or indirectly exclude such effects on the body, nor does reason exclude them.[59]

Through studying the history of revivals, Martyn Lloyd-Jones came to much the same conclusion:

> I would conclude that the phenomena are not essential to revival. . . . I believe that in their origin they are essentially of the Spirit of God, but we must always allow for the fact that because of the very frailty of human nature, and of our physical frames, you will have a tendency to an admixture, partly along the physical, partly along the psychic, and partly as the result of the Devil's activity. But there is nothing more foolish or more ridiculous than to dismiss the whole because of a very, very small

117

part. . . . [E]xpect this, and . . . be on guard against the false and spurious. . . . But we must not seek phenomena and strange experiences. . . . What we must seek is revival. . . . Anyone who tries to work up phenomena is a tool of the Devil, and is putting himself in the position of the psychic and the psychological.[60]

How then can people guard against deceiving spirits regarding such phenomena today? Two suggestions are recommended. First, A.B. Simpson's counsel from the first decade of the century is just as timely and timeless in the last decade as well: "In these days when the forces of heaven and hell are so intensely active, let us seek from God that gift which is of such practical value, the Spirit of discernment."[61] Secondly, Neil T. Anderson recommends the following prayer which bears repeating here:

Heavenly Father, I commit myself unreservedly to Your will. If I have been deceived in any way, I pray that You will open my eyes to the deception. I command in the name of the Lord Jesus Christ that all deceiving spirits depart from me, and I renounce and reject all counterfeit gifts (or any other spiritual phenomena). Lord, if it is from You, bless it and cause it to grow that Your body may be blessed and edified through it. Amen.[62]

If these guidelines are followed, we do not need to fear being deceived by counterfeit manifestations.

Endnotes

1 T.J. McCrossan, *Speaking in Other Tongues: Sign or Gift, Which?* (Harrisburg, PA: Christian Publications, 1927), 42.

2 Jonathan Edwards, "The Distinguishing Marks of the Work of the Spirit of God," *Jonathan Edwards on Revival* (Edinburgh: The Banner of Truth Trust, 1984), 91.

3 E.M. Bounds, *The Possibilities of Prayer* (Grand Rapids, MI: Baker Book House, 1979), 138.

4 Charles Finney, *The Autobiography of Charles Finney* (Minneapolis, MN: Bethany House, 1977), 22.

5 Mary N. Garrard, *Mrs. Penn-Lewis: A Memoir* (Hants, England: The Overcomer Book Room, 1947), 36-37.

6 A.B. Simpson, *Days of Heaven on Earth* (Camp Hill, PA: Christian Publications, 1984), June 27.

7 *Oswald Chambers: His Life and Work* (London: Simpkin Marshall, Ltd., 1947), 103.

8 Ibid., 104.

9 Ibid., 105.

10 Capt. E.G. Carre, ed., *Praying Hyde: A Challenge to Prayer* (Asheville, NC: Revival Literature, n.d.), 26.

11 Ibid., 31.

12 A.W. Tozer, *Worship: The Missing Jewel* (Camp Hill, PA: Christian Publications, 1992), 20-21.

13 Adolf Rodewyk, *Possessed by Satan*, trans. Martin Ebon (Garden City, NY: Doubleday, 1975), 152.

14 Jessie Penn-Lewis with Evan Roberts, *War on the Saints: Unabridged Edition* (New York: Thomas E. Lowe, Ltd., n.d.), 320, 324.

15 B.J. Oropeza, *A Time to Laugh: The Holy Laughter Phenomenon* (Peabody, MA: Hendrickson Publishers, 1995), 158.

16 John Wesley, *The Journal of John Wesley* (Chicago: Moody Press, n.d.), 76.

17 Edwards, 91-92. He gives as biblical examples the fainting of the queen of Sheba, the trembling and falling of the Philippian jailer, and others (pp. 91-94).

18 Finney, 100-101; also 23, 37, 46, 57-58, 63, 116, 120, 125, 131, 139, 163.

19 R.A. Torrey, *The Power of Prayer* (Grand Rapids, MI: Zondervan, 1971), 46-47.

20 Jonathan Goforth, *By My Spirit* (Minneapolis, MN: Bethany Fellowship, 1942, reprint 1964), 9-10.

21 W.A. Cramer, "Pentecost at Cleveland," *Christian and Missionary Alliance Weekly* 27 (April 27, 1907): 201; A.B. Simpson, "Editorial," *Christian and Missionary Alliance Weekly* 27 (June 8, 1907): 205; Stanley H. Frodsham, *With Signs Following*, rev. ed. (Springfield, MO: Gospel Publishing House, 1946), 51-52.

22 Maria Woodworth-Etter, *Acts of the Holy Ghost: The Life, Work, and Experience of Mrs. M.B. Woodworth-Etter* (Dallas, TX: John F. Worley Printing Co., n.d.), 354-355, 357, 369.

23 T.J. McCrossan, *Bodily Healing and the Atonement* (Youngstown, OH: Clement Hubbard, 1930), 109-110.

24 Charles S. Price, *See God* (Pasadena, CA: Charles S. Price Publishing House, 1943), 80; compare T.J. McCrossan, *Speaking with Other Tongues*, 34.

25 Finney, 21.

26 McCrossan, *Speaking with Other Tongues*, 46.

27 Irene E. Lewis, *Life Sketch of Rev. Mary C. Norton: Remarkable Healings on Mission Fields* (Los Angeles: Pilgrim's Mission, Inc., 1954), 27.

28 Ibid.

29 James A. Stewart, *Invasion of Wales by the Spirit* (Asheville, NC: Revival Literature, n.d.), 29.

30 Edwards, 64.

31 Ibid., 151.

32 Finney, 23, 163-164; Wesley, 76, 293.

33 Maria Woodworth-Etter wrote:

> A woman came to me and said, "I am afraid this spirit on me is not of God; I was baptized in the Holy Ghost; I went into a mission where they did everything by tongues and they got me so mixed up I did not know where I was; then this spirit got hold of me; it shakes my head and makes my head ache."
>
> That is spiritualism. Some people, when they pray for anyone and lay on hands, throw their slime off. That is spiritualism. . . . Be careful who lays hands on you, for the devil is counterfeiting God's work. (Woodworth-Etter, 508)

34 Carre, 23-24.

35 Oesterreich in his monumental work *Possession* writes of many examples of possession by animal spirits, such as cats, badgers, tiger, ox, dogs, monkeys, snakes, lions and foxes. T.K. Oesterreich, *Possession: Demonical and Other* (New Hyde Park, NY: University Books, 1966), 144-145. A person with a fox spirit, for instance, "adopts the habits of foxes" (224). A person with a tiger spirit would get on his hands and knees and growl (274-275). Another woman would glide like a snake and speak in tongues (144). He also records that a demon roared (184). In another instance, St. Francis cast out roaring demons (182). Jerome reports in his biography of St. Paula that possessed persons in Samaria "howled like wolves, barked like dogs, roared like lions, hissed like serpents, bellowed like bulls." (162). In Algiers dancers are possessed and imitate voices of lions and camels (263). In another instance, a monkey spirit caused a child to swing to and fro and to climb supernaturally. (276).

John Wesley also spoke of roaring taking place in demonized people. Frederick S. Leahy, *Satan Cast Out* (Edinburgh: The Banner of Truth Trust, 1975), 121. Nineteenth-century Presbyterian missionary John Nevius writes of demons with a voice like a bird (46) and twisting of body. John L. Nevius, *Demon Possession and Allied Themes* (Chicago: Fleming H. Revell, n.d.), 53. Johann Christoph Blumhardt describes a demon roaring during deliverance. McCandlish Phillips, *The Bible, the Supernatural, and the Jews* (Minneapolis: Bethany House, 1970), 199.

36   A.B. Simpson, *Christian and Missionary Alliance Weekly*, Feb. 2, 1907.

37   Charles Parham, *The Everlasting Gospel* (Baxter Springs, n.d.), 71-72.

38   Woodworth-Etter, 507-508.

39   Garry Friesen with Robin Maxson, *Decision Making and the Will of God* (Portland, OR: Multnomah, 1980), 127ff.

40   A.T. Pierson, *George Müller of Bristol* (New York: Fleming H. Revell, 1899), 134-135.

41   Carre, 22.

42   Torrey, 48.

43   Stewart, 31-33, 36, 43, 46, 51, 61, 76.

44   A.W. Tozer, *Wingspread* (Camp Hill, PA: Christian Publications, 1943), 62.

45   George Pardington, *Twenty-five Wonderful Years* (New York: Christian Alliance Publishing Co., 1914), 216.

46   Louise Green, "Robert Jaffray: Man of Spirit, Man of Power," *His Dominion*, 16:1, 10-11.

47   C.H. Gootee, "The Miracle of My Healing," *Triumphs of Faith* (March 1926), 62.

48   For instance, Maria Woodworth-Etter, who circulated both in holiness and early Pentecostal circles, advised, "Don't take up with every vision that comes along." She gave an example of one such spurious revelation: "In the midst of a vision she heard a voice say to her 'You are going to die.' But it was the devil." Woodworth-Etter, 503, 506.

49   Carrie Judd Montgomery, *The Life and Teaching of Carrie Judd Montgomery: Under His Wings* (New York: Garland Publishing, Inc., 1985), 159-161.

50   Martin Wells Knapp, *Impressions* (Cincinnati: Revivalist Publishing House, 1892), 15.

51   Thomas Upham, *The Life of Faith* (New York: Garland Publishing, 1984 reprint Boston: Waite, Pierce, 1845), 85.

52   Knapp, 34.

53   Roberts and Penn-Lewis, 131.

[54] Ibid., 297-298.

[55] Ibid., 285.

[56] Green, 10-11, also Stewart, 29.

[57] Hank Hanegraaff, *Counterfeit Revival* (Dallas: Word Publishers, 1997).

[58] Wesley, 239.

[59] Edwards, 91.

[60] D. Martyn Lloyd-Jones, *Revival* (Wheaton, IL: Crossway Books, 1987), 146-147.

[61] Richard Gilbertson, *The Baptism of the Holy Spirit: The Views of A.B. Simpson and His contemporaries* (Camp Hill, PA: Christian Publications, 1993), 321-322.

[62] Neil T. Anderson, *The Bondage Breaker* (Eugene, OR: Harvest House Publisher, 1990, 1993), 165.

Implicit Christians:
An Evangelical Appraisal

K. Neill Foster

The theme of this paper centers on the concepts of implicit faith and implicit Christianity. Supported by analogical arguments and fueled by the modern revulsion to the severity of orthodoxy's traditional pronouncements on hell and judgment, implicit faith ideas seem to hold a certain fascination for evangelical scholars. The whole discussion relates directly to another major theme, the lostness of mankind.

The implicit terms are new; the ideas are not.

But first, a brief definition of implicit Christianity. Its positive assumptions are commendable: Jesus Christ is the only Savior. Mankind, being eternally lost, is in need of a Savior. Its negative assumptions produce anxiety: Some will gain eternal life without ever expressly confessing Jesus Christ, perhaps without even knowing His name. Some "holy" pagans may be saved without ever hearing the name of Jesus Christ. The formal label for this belief is inclusivism.

Hunter's Predictions

Sociologist James Davison Hunter's work, *Evangelicalism: The Coming Generation* predicts trends in the coming generation of evangelicals. The Virginia-based academic has warned, surprisingly, that salvation by works among the untold millions was seen, in 1987, as an increasingly viable option by a large percentage of evangelical students, perhaps as high as thirty-three percent. His work is based upon an attitudinal survey called the Evangelical Academy Project that surveyed the attitudes and views of faculty and students at sixteen well-known evangelical institutions of higher learning, nine liberal arts colleges and seven seminaries.[1]

Sharply Modified Universalism

If Hunter's research on this issue is as accurate as it has already demonstrated itself to be on the emerging openness of evangelicals to some hope for the untold, then what he says about the coming damage to the missionary motive is chilling:

> . . . only 67 percent [of evangelical collegians and seminarians] agreed that "unless missionaries and others are successful in converting people in non-Christian lands, these people will have no chance for salvation."[2]

Also take note: Hunter saw something else coming and early on caught the essence of salvation by works within the postulation of salvation for special cases among those who have never heard. The "virtuous pagans" who never hear of Jesus Christ but still would be saved under inclusivism are clearly to be "exemplary people whose lives were characterized by extraordinary good will and charity."[3]

As improbable as it may seem, Hunter in 1987 was describing an emerging evangelical propensity toward salvation by works among the children of the Reformation.

> For a substantial minority of the coming generation, there appears to be a middle ground that did not . . . exist for previous generations. For the unevangelized and for those *who reveal exceptional Christian virtue but are not professed Christians* [emphasis added], there is hope that they also will receive salvation. . . . Needless to say, this posture would, and in fact does lessen substantially the sense of urgency to evangelize the un-reached.[4]

D.A. Carson thinks inclusivism is "not far removed from the qualified universalism of Neal Punt."[5]

Hunter does not use the term implicit Christian to describe what he sees coming in the next generation of evangelicals. And though his primary illustration of the implicit tendency is the "second chance theory," he does, as we have just said, accurately describe emerging implicit faith concepts in the evangelical milieu: "For the unevangelized and *for those who reveal exceptional Christian virtue* [emphasis added] but are not professed Christians, there is hope that they also will receive salvation. " This he terms "universalism in a sharply modified form."[6]

Evangelical Penetration

John Sanders estimates that the percentage of evangelical students with affinities to inclusivism at InterVarsity's 1975 Urbana conference at twenty-five percent.[7] A more recent estimate suggests penetrations of inclusivism as high as fifty percent among denominational leaders and professors in "mainstream evangelical colleges and seminaries."[8]

The Pluralistic Tandem

Marching alongside the evangelical interest in inclusivism are some of the writings of John Hick[9] and Paul F. Knitter[10]. These men are pluralists who protest the uniqueness of Jesus Christ as the only Savior of the world. Sometimes the evangelical lurch toward inclusivism is propelled by their pluralistic arguments. And, indeed, evangelical inclusivists often try to legitimize their advocacy of implicit ideas as a response to Hick and Knitter.

Evert D. Osburn

Osburn has written one of the seminal essays on the new inclusivism. He says ". . . it seems unfair to many that millions of unreached people would be condemned by a just and loving God even though they have never had a chance to hear of Jesus."[11] And he clearly understands what he is saying. "If such a person were to *subsequently* [emphasis added] hear the gospel he would instinctively realize its truth."[12] Likewise, his summary is very clear, ". . . a sincere believer in the one true creator God may possibly be saved apart from explicit knowledge of the gospel of Christ."[13]

W. Gary Phillips

Phillips does not embrace the implicit concepts, but he has caught the essence of the implicit faith concept exceptionally well.

> This solution [implicit faith] offers a form of inclusivism which reasons that the redemption of the Untold takes place in this life (not in the future or in other possible present worlds), even though there is no explicit choice for Christ. . . . Since God redeemed those who had not heard (who were ignorant of Jesus through no fault of their own), would not God be consistent to extend his mercy also to the Untold . . . ?[14]

Later, he further describes the theologians of the implicit concept:

> . . . they believe that the weight of evidence plus inferences from the character of God (as both just and loving) favor "lenient" inclusivism. In the face of their Judge, some Untold will see their Savior.[15]

The question which immediately surfaces: Since these concepts bear little resemblance to the New Testament, where did these ideas come from?

Pelagius

The long answer is Pelagius, though there are traces of this in Justin Martyr and the Eastern Church.

In early Britain Pelagius began to postulate a form of salvation by works that roused the ire of Augustine. In a twenty-year polemic against Pelagius, Augustine followed the apostolic pattern set by Paul in his assault on Galatianism in the New Testament. Pelagius advocated "the idea that man can achieve salvation by cooperation with the divine will through his own efforts."[16] The word commonly used to describe Pelagianism is heresy.[17]

But, more directly, and more recently, where did these inclusivistic ideas now come from? The short answer is Vatican II.

Vatican II and Universalistic Inclusivism

What theologian Millard Erickson calls "universalistic inclusivism"[18] is clearly spelled out in the Vatican II documents. Though the documents fall decidedly short "of the pope's unqualified soteriological universalism,"[19] they still have had immense impact.

> Those [who have not yet received the gospel] also can attain to everlasting salvation who through no fault of their own do not know the gospel of Christ or His Church, yet sincerely seek God and, moved by grace, strive *by their deeds* [emphasis added] to do His will as it is known unto them through the dictates of conscience.[20]

It will be significant later in this paper to remember here that implicit ideas as part of what Erickson calls "universalistic inclusivism" and Hunter refers to as "universalism in a sharply modified form" and Phillips calls "lenient inclusivism" contain latent Galatianism, a propensity toward salvation by works.

Karl Rahner

Rahner is the Roman Catholic theologian who took some of the missiological ideas advocated in Vatican II and formulated a theology to accompany them.[21] His concepts of "anonymous Christians" and "baptism by desire"[22] became the forerunners of what is now being called implicit faith and implicit Christianity. Rahner's role is pivotal in that he took the latent universalism of Vatican II and popularized it.

Harold Netland

Netland supplies an interesting bit of background to this discussion when he observes that implicit ideas first gained some kind of evangelical credence when the Lausanne conference failed to repudiate inclusivism. According to Netland, "the Lausanne Covenant was framed in such a manner as to allow for some diversity of opinion on this point."[23]

The modern emergence of universalistic inclusivism among evangelicals has run an interesting route. Rooted in the Galatianism of the first century and the Pelagianism of the fourth, it was conceived anew in Vatican II. It was advanced by Rahner. It apparently escaped repudiation at Lausanne.

In recent times it has been embraced and advocated by Clark Pinnock and John Sanders.

David Hesselgrave

Describing inclusivism, though not by name, among "current trends and ideas" that Hudson Taylor and A.B. Simpson would find amazing, David Hesselgrave, the missiologist from Trinity Divinity School, in a recent issue of *Alliance Life* offers a definition of implicit Christianity as follows:

> The idea that all people who humbly and sincerely seek God [usually understood to be just a few] will be saved irrespective of whether or not they hear and believe in Jesus Christ.[24]

Millard Erickson

Erickson, for his part, specifically labels "implicit faith" as one kind of universalistic inclusivism.[25] Phillips' term "lenient inclusivism"[26] is a little weaker than Erickson's and fails to catch the universalistic nuances emerging from Vatican II and latent within the implicit ideas.

Clark Pinnock

Clark Pinnock is the best known of the implicit theologians.

His recent book, *A Wideness in God's Mercy*, argues against the biblical orthodoxy of past generations and for a much more relaxed view of the lostness of mankind.

> We have now refuted the restrictivist view that says that only those who actually confess Jesus in this life can be saved. . . . On the contrary, the Bible teaches that many varieties of unevangelized persons will attain salvation.[27]

In an article supportive of implicit faith concepts, Pinnock argues, almost tongue-in-cheek, against the commonly held evangelical view of Acts 4:12, i.e., that there is no other name under heaven, given among men, whereby we *must* be saved.[28]

His solution: the text refers to physical healing as well as salvation (and salvation does include healing), but he remains silent on the *must* of the text.

> There is a glaring omission in his [Pinnock's] treatment of this verse. Heresies are usually not so wrong in their admissions as they are in their omissions. Dr. Pinnock nowhere deals with the Greek word *dei* or "must" in this verse. Billy Graham says that many want to leave this same word "must" *dei* out of John 3:7, where our Lord says, "You must *dei* be born again."[29]

Perhaps because of his admitted bias[30] Pinnock adopts inclusivist hermeneutics and turns the words of Peter upside down. As Tozer observed on the subject of such zig-zag hermeneutics, "Casuistry is not the possession of Roman Catholic theologians alone."[31]

John Sanders

As a student of Pinnock, Sanders has written one of the key books on the wider hope. We find him exulting that "inclusivism has representatives from a broader cross-section of the church than any other wider-hope view."[32]

Key Arguments

Several conceptual ideas travel with universalistic inclusivism.

- In the Old Testament, the tendency is to consider Melchizedek a holy pagan, rather than someone who has had a direct revelation of God or has come to know Yahweh through Abraham.[33]
- In the New Testament Cornelius is thought to be the perfect example of a holy pagan. That Peter went to Cornelius and explained to him *the words by which he was saved* (Acts 11:14) is an unacceptable explanation.[34] That the Scriptures clearly say that *Cornelius had to receive saving words* is repeatedly ignored by inclusivists. There is a distressing tendency latent within inclusivism to relieve the Church of its obligation to preach the gospel to the Jews, because if holy pagans can be saved, why cannot Jewish inquirers come to the Father under the Old Covenant? If a faith-path without the Savior can be found in the Old Testament, a mediator will not then be needed. Inclusivism has large regard for the Old Covenant but a deliberately fuzzy conception of the New Covenant.[35]
- There is a strong hope among inclusivists that natural revelation will have saving effect, that the lost may indeed be saved by looking at nature and concluding that there must be a Creator/Savior.
- The hermeneutics of inclusivism are indirect and elastic.[36] The plain sense of many of the New Testament statements flies directly in the face of inclusivism.[37] The imperative texts such as John 3:3-7; 14:6; Acts 4:12; Ephesians 2:3, 8-10 and Romans 10 have to be softened, skirted or omitted to make inclusivism work.
- There are necessarily strong appeals made to rationalism made in inclusivism. If God saved people in the Old Testament before the advent of Jesus Christ, why will He not save in the same way today, especially when the persons in-

volved have never heard of Jesus Christ? Analogy and logic, legitimate though they be, take precedence over exegesis in the framing of inclusivism's appeal.[38]

Cairns has observed that "Error is perennial and usually springs from the same causes in every age. Man's pride in reason and his rationalizing tendency can still lead to heresy as it did in the Colossian church."[39]

- Sometimes inclusivist thinking suggests that allowing for implicit Christians is no different than believing in God's acceptance of the mentally retarded or children before the age of accountability. That "implicit Christians" are by definition *accountable* sinners who have broken God's law and are without excuse (Romans 1:20) is conveniently forgotten.
- Finally, in inclusivism rigid exegetical procedures must be abandoned since they will not carry anyone to an unbiblical result.[40]

Is Inclusivism Heresy?

Is it error to affirm the existence of implicit Christians? Is implicit Christianity heresy? A number of careful questions need to be asked about implicit Christians.

A third and highly significant question relates to the worldwide missionary enterprise. If there are possibly some who will be saved without ever hearing the name of Jesus Christ, is the cord of missionary urgency being cut? Hick, the pluralist, acknowledges one major result of inclusivism "is that it negates the old missionary compulsion. . . ."[41] Hunter has already shown that such a negation is presently taking place.

> Needless to say, this posture . . . [i.e., some hope for the Untold] does lessen substantially the sense of urgency to evangelize the unreached.[42]

When comparing seminarians who believe that "Jesus is the only way for salvation except for those who have not heard of Jesus" with those who believe that "Jesus is the only way period" on a number of items, a pattern was found to hold true. For example, the former were less likely to hold evangelism as the highest priority in the church, more likely to believe that social justice is "just as important" or "almost as important" as evangelism and *much less likely to choose missions as a career path—by two to one* [emphasis added].[43]

As this argumentation proceeds, the terms "implicit Christian" and "implicit faith" are used in synonymous ways, although the first tends in part to be Christological and the second almost wholly soteriological. The first is rooted in Roman Catholicism; the second is obviously a persuasive adaptation for Protestants and evangelicals who are thought to still value highly the results of the Reformation. The general subject, of course, is universalistic inclusivism.

Taking a Cue from Bowman

At this point, taking a cue from Bowman,[44] my object is to cast a number of principles in bold relief against the concept of implicit Christianity. The procedure, I find, is very helpful in making a decision about the real danger and inherent nature of any kind of error.

1) *The Protestant Principle.* Is implicit Christianity supported by the Protestant Principle of *Sola Scriptura*? The answer is that analogical arguments and rational processes create implicit faith and implicit Christians. Apart from devious hermeneutics, Scripture does not. Nash properly calls it "biblically unsupportable opinion."[45] Inclusivists do claim Scriptural support, but the refutation of those claims is a book-length project in itself and beyond the scope of this paper.

2) *The Grace Principle.* The New Testament, evangelicals believe, teaches that salvation is not of works, but by grace through faith (Ephesians 2:8-9). Earlier we observed that sociologist Hunter was predicting the evangelical abandonment of

the grace principle on the basis of studies done in various colleges. If implicit Christians are those who turn from their idols to serve the God whose name they do not know and need not know, are they not receptors of grace through explicit works? Is implicit Christianity anything other than latent Galatianism?

A common trait of inclusivists is a persistent failure to see that their advocacy of implicit ideas ultimately involves salvation by works. Good works are expected from holy pagans who have never received the life-changing gospel and who have never had more than general revelation to guide them.

Nash observes essentially that about John Sanders.

> Once again we confront an issue on which it appears the inclusivists want to walk down both sides of that street at the same time. On the one hand, John Sanders takes the historic evangelical position that no humans "are saved by their own moral efforts."[46] On the other hand, he ignores inclusivist implications to the exact opposite.[47]

Pinnock likewise has fallen into the same error of trying to embrace, at once, both evangelical doctrine and universalistic inclusivism.

> Surely God judges the heathen in relation to the light they have, not according to the light that did not reach them. Of course God condemns those who really are his enemies. But his judgment will take into account what people are conscious of, what they yearn for, what they have suffered, *what they do* [emphasis added] out of love, and so forth.[48]

Nash observes that "Pinnock is suggesting that a person who lacks New Testament faith but produces good works of a certain kind may still be saved on that basis."[49]

John Sanders demonstrates this tendency again in a recent issue of the *Christian Scholar's Review*. Since implicit Christians do not confess Jesus Christ, we find him affirming that "effective action is the proper response to God's grace" for implicit Christians but wishing for "public badges" which he admits remain "elusive."[50]

When the agenda ideas of universalistic inclusivism play themselves out, the advocacy of implicit Christianity and implicit faith involves salvation by works. The implicit Christianity of inclusivism is contrary to both Galatians and Ephesians. It is just as error-laden as Galatianism or Pelagianism ever were.

Interestingly enough, some inclusivists seem not to realize that implicit Christianity ultimately includes salvation by works. One of the reasons may be that in 1990 inclusivism took the field first. Pinnock and Sanders were published first. Richard has argued against them effectively, but Nash is really the first to take them on in a public collision. As Brown has observed, orthodoxy may be expected to take the field of battle late in any case.[51] The emerging attacks on inclusivism will assault the implicit ideas. Once it becomes clear under the pressure of critical scrutiny that implicit Christians have to become holy pagans to be saved by works, the violation of the grace principle will be seen as well.

3) *The Name Principle.* After Pentecost, Luke observes in Acts that the disciples began to minister in the name of Jesus Christ. At the gate of the temple Peter and John healed in the name (3:6). The religious authorities were aware that the lame man, more than forty years old, had been made whole in the name of Jesus (4:10). Peter's sermon includes the classic words, "Salvation is found in no one else, for there is no other name under heaven given to men by which we must be saved" (4:12). When threats were issued to the empowered Church, they were told to desist using the name (4:18). Their decision was to continue to use the name because the Holy Spirit, they had already learned, was given to the obedient (5:32). They risked their lives to use the name.

By way of contrast, the implicitists who follow the universalism of Vatican II at a distance tell us that the name of Jesus

Christ is not important for at least a few. Some will be receptors of grace and saved whether or not they ever get to know the name (Sanders, Osburn, Pinnock, etc.). Implicit faith for implicit Christians rides roughshod over the name. Worse, when exceptions are made which supposedly allow some to circumvent the name and still be saved, the name of Jesus Christ is by that measure diminished.

4) *The Covenental Principle.* One of the key ways that implicit faith advocates advance their arguments is through appeals to the Old Testament. And this is not bad in itself since Christians are to learn from what happened in the Old Testament (1 Corinthians 10:6, 11). However, to ignore the New Covenant (and the whole book of Hebrews) is surely serious business. Christ is the mediator of that covenant (Hebrews 9:15). Are there not at least two different ways God deals with man? The Old Testament and the New Testament? The Old Covenant and the New Covenant? The Old Covenant was made obsolete by the New Covenant (8:13). Jesus said at the last supper, "This cup is the new covenant in my blood, which is poured out for you" (Luke 22:20).

Implicit faith advocates are immensely attracted to the ways God worked before Christ came. Those arguments are summoned to support implicit faith and implicit Christianity. Is despite (Hebrews 10:29, KJV) being done to the blood of the New Covenant at the same time?

Jewish ministries have been appalled at implications by "evangelical" theologians that it is no longer necessary for Jews to believe in Jesus Christ to be saved.[52] Arthur F. Glasser believes that Wilson, in his book, *Our Father Abraham*, creates a "mood that will increasingly overtake the reader's consciousness as he or she presses on deeper and deeper into this book: *The church has no business evangelizing Jews*" [emphasis added].[53]

Like implicit faith and implicit Christianity, the "evangelical" retreat from salvation for Jews apart from an explicit faith in Jesus Christ seeks to find its rationale in a Messiah-free faith-path supposedly still found in the Old Testament. Not incidentally, salvation for Jews apart from Jesus Christ shares one common feature with the inclusivism of implicit faith and implicit Christianity. Both circumnavigate the bulwark texts in John 3, John 14, Acts 4, Ephesians 2 and Romans 10 and in the case of Jewish ministries, Romans 1:16, "to the Jew first."

The validity of the New Testament and the uniqueness of Jesus Christ as the only mediator between God and man are antithetical to the message of salvation for Jews apart from Jesus Christ. These same concepts are likewise, in a very close parallel, antithetical to the implicit faith and implicit Christian concepts of universalistic inclusivism.

5) *The Consequential Principle.* Is the implicit Christian concept error in view of its consequences? Krumm suggests that differences in viewpoints are often held in the Church, until it is perceived that a viewpoint has consequential peril. Then it becomes heresy.[54] Can implicit faith be a dangerous view? All one has to do is apply small doses of rationalism, logic and philosophy and one has annulled the great evangelistic texts and compromised the missionary mandate. The result is what Radmacher calls "hermeneutical leakage."[55]

At risk in the implicit-Christian view is the authority and integrity of Jesus Christ and Scripture, the declarations of Peter and Paul, the lostness of mankind and the necessity of obedience to the Great Commission.

At risk, ultimately, is the uniqueness of Jesus Christ.

If inclusivism finally and fully gets the heresy label, it will get it first from the evangelical missiologists. Universalistic inclusivism is at its roots, in destructive collision with the missionary mandate.

It is important to observe that these issues are not static. The evangelical appraisal of inclusivism is ongoing. Likewise, heresy, as it leavens and expands itself, is finally self-condemned according to Scripture (Titus 3:10-11), i.e., there is betraying movement inherent in it. That is why universalistic inclusivism bears watching. That is why waiting is necessary (2 Timothy 4:2-4). In the seven years that I have been focused on this issue, and coincidental with an expanding interest in the subject, I have become aware that in some parts, at least, there is a stiffen-

136

ing evangelical resolve against inclusivism. We are finding out what it means and where it takes us.

The consequential principle may be the principle which finally pins a heresy label on this kind of universalism in miniature. The price of allowing it free flow as a valid "evangelical option" may have already become too high, i.e., the "negation of the old missionary compulsion."[56]

6) *The Hermeneutical Principle.* Implicit Christianity advances on novel hermeneutics. If one holds to the grammatical-historical method of interpretation, if one clings to the Protestant hermeneutic of the Reformation, i.e., comparing Scripture with Scripture, the traditional evangelistic texts hold. Implicit faith and implicit Christian ideas get nowhere with these texts resolutely blocking their advance.

However, if these texts must be circumnavigated (and they must be for universalistic inclusivism to be embraced), then the hermeneutical dance begins. There are cultural hermeneutics, anthropological hermeneutics, archeological hermeneutics, even unconscious hermeneutics. There is certainly the hermeneutic of inclusivism. The more frenzied the hermeneutical dance, the more distant from truth the interpretation becomes. Note carefully, implicit faith and implicit Christian interpretations require elaborate dances, the artful explaining away of the bulwark texts. Pinnock's exercise on Acts 4:12 where he ignores the obligatory power of the Greek *dei*[57] illustrates the hermeneutical dance exactly.

Arnold L. Cook, president of The Christian and Missionary Alliance in Canada, recently addressed the hermeneutical issue as it relates to the biblical understanding of hell. His comments on "tampering hermeneutics" are equally appropriate when the subject is inclusivism.

> On this slippery slope, these theologians are tampering with the clear teaching of the Scriptures. They are trying to prop up God's justice while yielding to the subjectivity of their feelings.
> . . . These proponents, well-intentioned though they

be, are unknowingly embracing a low view of Scripture. They are moving the church backwards into the pre-Vatican II days of 1962-1965, and perhaps even back to pre-Reformation days. I refer to those times when ordinary Christians supposedly could not understand, [even] with the Holy Spirit's help, the plain truth of Scripture. These theologians are allowing scholarship to obscure the clear views of Scripture on these subjects. Ordinary believers are intimidated and question, "Can we no longer understand the Bible by just reading it with the Spirit's help, comparing Scripture with Scripture?"[58]

An illustration of the hermeneutics of inclusivism is offered by Erickson, who is citing Knitter.

At the heart of this endeavor is Knitter's hermeneutic. He follows Hans George Gadamer's concept that every text has two horizons—that of the author and that of the reader. In Knitter's adaptation, it is not sufficient to interpret a text within its historical context. Both the text and its context can be understood only "within the 'horizon' of experience and meaning" as that horizon expands through history.[59]

Knitter himself argues, "Unless the text and its context are continually being reheard in the ever new texture, one is really not hearing what the text means."[60]

This elasticized hermeneutic fails to recognize any deposit of faith, any message "once for all entrusted to the saints" (Jude 3).

If the idea of implicit Christians is further advanced, look for elasticized hermeneutical maneuvering and novel interpretations on Romans 10:9-15 to appear in the implicit literature. Sanders has already begun the elasticizing process on that passage.[61] Itinerant hermeneutics, always flexible, are the essential tools of the universalistic inclusivist.

The early creeds of the Church, which have hermeneutical implications as well, were theological constructs meant to keep heresies at bay. While we cannot attribute scriptural authority to the creeds, they offer no comfort to the inclusivism inherent in implicit faith and implicit Christian ideas.

7) *The Soteriological Principle.* Salvation comes in some way to mankind. Universalistic inclusivists do not deny that salvation comes through Jesus Christ. What they deny is that the name of Jesus Christ must be known by the lost person (cf. Acts 4:12). They also deny that the lost person must openly call upon the name of the Lord (cf. Romans 10:9-13). Just a very few will enter the kingdom of God without these biblical prerequisites. But, they say, a few will. If any kind of repentance takes place it would apparently be implicit as well. This form of "lenient" inclusivism must circumnavigate the bulwark evangelistic texts.

8) *The Inclusion/Omission Principle.* Error is often known for what it fails to say, for what it leaves out and omits as much as for what it does say. Adherence to implicit faith requires certain omissions, notably the bulwark texts we have been discussing.

In describing Satan's selective quotation of Scripture to Jesus Christ, A. B. Simpson astutely observes,

> Satan . . . left out seven words in the quotation of the 91st Psalm. . . . You may always distinguish between the right and wrong use of Scripture by this text. The devil uses the Bible too, but he uses it dishonestly to establish some special theory and without regard to the other Scriptures which appear upon the same point. We must remember always, not only that it is written (Matthew 4:4), *"but that it is also written"* [emphasis added] (4:5).[62]

Inclusivist literature tends to omit key biblical passages. Romans 10 is frequently omitted since it is the most difficult to bend to inclusivist theory. John's Gospel and his epistles are also uncomfortable territory for inclusivists.

9) *The Gospel Principle.* Universalistic inclusivists decline to focus intently on Jesus Christ. Implicit faith, it is assumed, may be directed to something or someone other than Jesus Christ. "People can receive the gift of salvation without knowing the

giver or the precise nature of the gift."[63] For his part, Pinnock says openly, "According to the Bible, people are saved by faith, not by the content of their theology."[64]

These affirmations, and many like them, run aground on such passages as First Corinthians 15:3-4 where the gospel is enunciated as belief in Christ's death, burial and resurrection. If faith is unfocused, then inclusivism seems to posit faith in faith, reminiscent of the word of faith teachers of today. If indeed universalistic inclusivism is preached as a gospel, then the apostle Paul must be reckoned with. In Second Corinthians 11 he warns against another Jesus, a different spirit, a different gospel from the one accepted by the Corinthians. Universalistic inclusivism qualifies rather well as an alternate gospel. Nash believes J.I. Packer, in a veiled reference, is calling Pinnock's universalistic inclusivism exactly that, "a new gospel."[65] Also note, the false apostles' gospel of Second Corinthians 11 goes down rather well with some of the Corinthians. It was smooth—they put up with it "easily enough" (11:4). The smoothness of inclusivism ought to raise doctrinal alarms quickly. Sound doctrine, after all, has sharp edges to it and has to be endured (2 Timothy 4:3). Universalistic inclusivism is too, too plausible, too, too reasonable to qualify as truth or sound doctrine. Rather, it sounds uncomfortably like another gospel, another Jesus (if ever his name be really known) and another spirit.

10) *The Heresy Principle.* Heresy, as we realize, means a party spirit, disunion, to divide (2 Timothy 4:2-4, KJV). Also, Paul makes clear, heresies serve the purpose of showing who is who in the Church. Some have God's approval and some do not (1 Corinthians 11:19). Heresies "must come" and of course they do, everywhere the gospel is preached. Paul's Philippian references to the defense of the gospel demonstrate that as soon as the good news lands, the defense must begin (1:7, 16, 27; 4:3). The apostle also reminds us that heresy is a work of the flesh (Galatians 5:20). And for his part, Peter calls heresies "destructive" and "damnable" (2 Peter 2:1, NIV, KJV).

If, as we insist, orthodoxy is preached here in North America, is it not reasonable to expect also that heresies will emerge? The answer is self-evident in the land of Mormons, Jehovah's Witnesses, Christian Science, the Family, the Branch Davidians and more. How about universalistic inclusivism for the academically inclined? Surely it appeals to the flesh as much as it divides. For damnation potential, how about billions who may never hear in a post-missionary era ruled by "evangelical" inclusivism?

Fortunately, and in correct order, since orthodoxy weighs into the battle after heresy begins to flower, the apologists are emerging to defend orthodoxy.[66] If there is no peril, why the alarm?

11) *The Christological Principle.* What do the implicit faith and implicit Christian concepts do to Jesus Christ? How does universalistic inclusivism relate to Christ? Is His absolute uniqueness at all eroded? Harold O.J. Brown's definition of heresy is that it "undercuts thievery basis for Christian existence." He goes on to add: "Practically speaking, heresy [involves] the doctrine of God and the doctrine of Christ—later called 'special theology' and 'Christology.' "[67]

Do these new concepts minimize open belief in His name? When implicit faith says that some of those who have never heard do not have to actively profess faith in Christ, can they be saved without knowing Him? And if so, do not then the words of Christ become of no effect? Is He any longer the only way to the Father?

If for some, the knowledge of His sacrificial death will not matter, does Jesus Christ still matter quite so much? Has His person, uniqueness and character been shrunken just one iota? Do not the implicit faith and implicit Christian ideas undercut the very essence of the missionary mandate?

Has not Christ's blood been "slightly" discounted? Has not "moderate" despite been done unto the Spirit of Grace (Hebrews 10:29, KJV)? God forbid.

Is the urgency and necessity of His sacrifice quite as imperative as it was before Karl Rahner[68] postulated anonymous Christians? If the implicit Christian idea clearly tampers with the uniqueness and finality of Jesus Christ as it certainly does, is it not then

Christological error? The implicit brand of inclusivism is not kind to Jesus Christ.

J. Christy Wilson, Jr.'s unpublished discussion of implicit faith ideas zeroes in on the Christological issue:

> In facing a similar heresy in Galatians, the apostle Paul writes, "If righteousness could be gained through the law, Christ died for nothing" Gal. 2:21b. The descriptions of "implicit Christians" . . . say that they have to live good lives. What is this but a form of salvation by works? *Thus it makes the cross of Christ of no effect and involves Christological error* [emphasis added].[69]

An Enormous Issue

Evangelicals are facing an issue of incalculable importance. Phillips was surely understating when he admitted that inclusivism might "become a watershed issue among evangelicals."[70] Nash observes that "The acceptance of this biblically unsupported opinion [inclusivism] carries an enormously high theological cost."[71] Netland likewise says, "The implications of this question are staggering."[72] Richard Ramesh even wonders if evangelicalism can survive inclusivism.[73]

William Carey once stood and declared that something should be done for the heathen. Though perhaps no one at the time realized it, the two greatest centuries of Christian mission in the history of the world had begun.

Similarly, Vatican II and the evangelical softness which has followed it may mark the end of the parenthesis we call the modern missionary movement. If our Lord delays His return, the twenty-first century may be the first century of the post-missionary era. We dare not forget that Hick is assuring us that inclusivism will certainly "negate the old missionary compulsion."[74]

Conclusion

Evangelicals have had some difficulty labeling implicit Christian ideas. Some earlier material[75] seems to welcome the camel of inclusivism into the evangelical tent. However, as time has gone on, the number of influential evangelicals willing to call implicit Christianity and universalistic inclusivism heresy has grown. The evidence is clearly overwhelming and multiplying. Hopefully, the result will be the wholesale abandonment of error.

Implicit Christianity is an heretical idea. It is unbiblical at its core. It is a Christological error. It is a soteriology driven by rationalism and suspect hermeneutics. It strikes at the vital nerve of missionary endeavor. Once the existence of even one implicit Christian is affirmed, implicit Christianity has moved from heretical thinking to heresy. Holy pagans invariably are going to have to exhibit good works to be saved. Galatianism, the undeniable heresy, will have re-emerged, among evangelicals no less, as universalistic inclusivism.

Endnotes

1 James Davison Hunter, *Evangelicalism: The Coming Generation* (Chicago: University of Chicago Press, 1987), 9.

2 Ibid., 36.

3 Ibid., 37.

4 Ibid., 47.

5 D.A. Carson, *The Gagging of God* (Grand Rapids, MI: Zondervan, 1996), 280.

6 Hunter, *Evangelicalism*, 47.

7 John Sanders, *No Other Name* (Grand Rapids, MI: Eerdmans, 1992), 216.

8 Ronald H. Nash, *Is Jesus the Only Savior?* (Grand Rapids, MI: Zondervan, 1994), 107.

9 John Hick and Paul F. Knitter, eds., *The Myth of Christian Uniqueness* (Maryknoll, NY: Orbis, 1987).

10 Paul F. Knitter, *No Other Name?* (Maryknoll, NY: Orbis, 1989).

11 Evert D. Osburn, "Those Who Have Never Heard: Have They No Hope?" *Journal of the Evangelical Theological Society* 32/3 September 1989, 367.

12 Ibid., 368.

13 Ibid., 372.

14 W. Gary Phillips, "Evangelicals and Pluralism: Current Options" *The Evangelical Quarterly* 64/3, 1992, 236-237.

[15] Ibid., 244.

[16] Earle E. Cairns, *Christianity Through the Centuries* (Grand Rapids, MI: Zondervan, 1954), 149.

[17] Roger Nicole, "New Testament Use of the Old," *Revelation and the Bible* (Grand Rapids, MI: Baker, 1958), 43.

[18] Millard Erickson, *The Word Became Flesh* (Grand Rapids, MI: Baker, 1991), 28-29.

[19] David Wright, "The Watershed of Vatican II: Catholic Approaches to Religious Pluralism" *One God, One Lord* (Grand Rapids, MI: Baker, 1992), 213.

[20] Walter M. Abbott, *The Documents of Vatican II* (New York: Guild Press, 1966), 35.

[21] Karl Rahner, *Theological Investigations*, Vol. 6 (New York: Seabury, 1969), 340-398.

[22] Erickson, *The Word Became Flesh*, 284.

[23] Harold Netland, *Dissonant Voices* (Grand Rapids, MI: Eerdmans, 1993), 265.

[24] David Hesselgrave, "The Alliance in the Spotlight" *Alliance Life*, May 26, 1993, 7.

[25] Millard Erickson, "The State of the Question," *Through No Fault of Their Own?* (Grand Rapids, MI: Baker, 1991), 28-29.

[26] Phillips, "Evangelicals and Pluralism," 244.

[27] Clark H. Pinnock, *A Wideness in God's Mercy* (Grand Rapids, MI: Zondervan, 1992), 168.

[28] Clark H. Pinnock, "Acts 4:12-No Other Name under Heaven," *Through No Fault of Their Own?* (Grand Rapids, MI: Baker, 1991), 107-115.

[29] J. Christy Wilson (Unpublished paper, 1993), 5.

[30] Pinnock, *Through No Fault of Their Own?*, 112.

[31] A.W. Tozer, *The Waning Authority of Christ in the Church* (Camp Hill, PA: Christian Publications, 1963), 2.

[32] Sanders, *No Other Name*, 274.

[33] Nash, *Is Jesus the Only Savior?*, 128.

[34] Bruce Demarest, *General Revelation* (Grand Rapids, MI: Zondervan, 1982), 191.

[35] Marvin R. Wilson, *Our Father Abraham* (Grand Rapids, MI: Eerdmans; Dayton, OH: Center for Judaic-Christian Studies, 1989).

[36] John Sanders, *No Other Name* (Grand Rapids, MI: Eerdmans, 1992), 246-247.

37 Nash, *Is Jesus the Only Savior?*, 145.

38 Pinnock, *A Wideness in God's Mercy*; Sanders, *No Other Name*.

39 Cairns, *Christianity Through the Centuries*, 73.

40 Nash, *Is Jesus the Only Savior?*, 175.

41 John Hick, *God & the Universe of Faiths* (Rockport, MA: Oneworld Publications, 1993), 143.

42 Hunter, *Evangelicalism*, 47.

43 Ibid., 258.

44 Robert M. Bowman, *Orthodoxy and Heresy* (Grand Rapids, MI: Baker, 1992).

45 Nash, *Is Jesus the Only Savior?*, 175.

46 Sanders, *No Other Name*, 235.

47 Nash, *Is Jesus the Only Savior?*, 169.

48 Clark Pinnock, *Theological Crossfire: An Evangelical-Liberal Debate* (Grand Rapids, MI: Zondervan, 1990), 367-368.

49 Nash, *Is Jesus the Only Savior?*, 170.

50 John Sanders, "Evangelical Responses to Salvation Outside the Church" *Christian Scholar's Review* xxiv: I, September 1994, 55.

51 Harold O.J. Brown, *Heresies* (Garden City, New York: Doubleday, 1984), 4.

52 Marvin R. Wilson, *Our Father Abraham*.

53 Arthur F. Glasser, "A Review of Our Father Abraham," for Lausanne Committee for Jewish Evangelism, 1991, 7.

54 John M. Krumm, *Modern Heresies* (Greenwich, CT: Seabury Press, 1961), 11.

55 Earl D. Radmacher and Robert D. Prues, eds., *Hermeneutics, Inerrancy, and the Bible* (Grand Rapids, MI: Zondervan, 1984), xii-xiii.

56 Hick, *God & the Universe of Faiths*, 143.

57 Pinnock, *Through No Fault of Their Own?*, 107-115.

58 Arnold L. Cook, *Remembering Those for Whom No Table Has Yet Been Set* (Toronto: The Christian & Missionary Alliance, 1994), 9.

59 Erickson, *The Word Became Flesh*, 284.

60 Knitter, *No Other Name?* 172.

61 Sanders, *No Other Name*, 67.

62 A.B. Simpson, *Christ in the Bible Commentary*, vol. 1 (Camp Hill, PA: Christian Publications, Inc., 1992), 28.

[63] Sanders, *No Other Name*, 224-225.

[64] Pinnock, *A Wideness in God's Mercy*, 157.

[65] Nash, *Is Jesus the Only Savior?*, 132.

[66] Larry Dixon, *The Other Side of the Good News* (Wheaton: Victor Books, 1992); Richard Ramesh, *The Population of Heaven* (Chicago: Moody, 1994); Nash, *Is Jesus the Only Savior?*

[67] Brown, *Heresies*, 2-3.

[68] Rahner, *Theological Investigations*, 340-398.

[69] J. Christy Wilson, Jr. (Unpublished paper, 1993), 11.

[70] Phillips, "Evangelicals and Pluralism," 242.

[71] Nash, *Is Jesus the Only Savior?*, 175.

[72] Netland, *Dissonant Voices*, 277.

[73] Ramesh, *The Population of Heaven*, 12.

[74] Hick, *God & the Universe of Faiths*, 143.

[75] Malcolm J. McVeigh, "The Fate of Those Who've Never Heard? It Depends." *Evangelical Mission Quarterly*, October 1985.

About the Authors

Elio Cuccaro, Ph.D. is Professor of Theology and Ministry at Nyack College, Nyack, NY and Senior Editor at Christian Publications, Camp Hill, PA.

K. Neill Foster, Ph.D. is Executive Vice President and Publisher of Christian Publications, the publishing house of The Christian and Missionary Alliance.

Doug Haskins is a licensed minister of The Christian and Missionary Alliance ministering in the Native American District in Flagstaff, AZ.

Rev. Paul L. King is pastor of the Tulsa Alliance Church, Tulsa, OK.

Douglas Matthews, Ph.D. is Associate Professor of Philosophy and Theology at Toccoa Falls College, Toccoa Falls, GA.

Timothy C. Tennent, Th.M. was until recently Assistant Professor of World Missions at Toccoa Falls College, Toccoa Falls, GA.

Joel Van Hoogen is a licensed minister of The Christian and Missionary Alliance now based in Boise, ID, presently serving as Director of Church Partnership Evangelism, a short-term ministry application for Alliance missions.